TRUE
TO
MYSELF

PEACE, LOVE, MARNI

MARNI GOLDMAN

Marni Goldman/True To Myself
Printed in the United States of America

True To Myself/ Marni Goldman -- 1st ed.

ISBN 9781710056853 Print Edition

CONTENTS

God Thinks I'm A Badass…And God Thinks You Are, Too! 1

Here for A Reason 5

Never, Ever Give Up 19

"Just Find A Rich Man" (Wait – What???) 41

The Ego Wants, But the Soul Needs 57

Love and Guilt Are Not the Same 81

All That Glitters Is Not Gold 103

Unzipping Myself 119

From Sour Lemons To Perfect Lemonade (The Making Of Peace, Love, Marni) 147

Being Unf***Withable 173

Marnivational Moments 185

Appendix: Resources 199

Acknowledgments 203

To anyone reading this,

Embrace the journey, Trust the universe, Stay strong, Believe in yourself, Love yourself, and Never give give up!

CHAPTER 1

GOD THINKS I'M A BADASS...*AND GOD THINKS YOU ARE, TOO!*

IT WAS MAY 1987. I had just turned 17. I didn't have a home, which meant I didn't have any place to celebrate my birthday. My mother's on-again, off-again "sugar daddy" boyfriend, a relatively decent guy named Milton, had just kicked us out of the apartment he'd been paying for in Aventura, Florida. He'd had enough, I guess, and I couldn't blame him. My mother had recently taken up with a crack addict named Michael—a complete and total loser who would later become her fifth husband—and was now addicted to crack herself.

Mom and I had nowhere else to go, so we spent the night at a Howard Johnson's. I wandered into the lounge and caught a stand-up comedy act. Laughing at the one-liners cheered me; I couldn't stop cracking up. After the show, the comedian, who was just a few years older than me, hung out with me a bit, talking and laughing some more. That was great, but when it was over, I went back upstairs to the room where my mother was sleeping. I sat on the bed staring at her, realizing that humor, that putting my troubles out of my mind temporarily, was all well and good, but it wouldn't change my family's circumstances.

The next night, my mother and I planned to move to another

motel. Michael was joining us, much to my disgust. I knew he was on crack, and I avoided him like the plague.

We stopped at a gas station off I-95 and Hollywood Boulevard. I was driving a red Pontiac Firebird, my pride and joy. Mom and Michael were in his beat-up car. My clothes and all my other belongings were stuffed into the backseat of my Firebird. It wasn't much, but it was all I had in the world.

After I'd filled up, Michael came over and told me to unlock the driver's-side door. I refused.

"Then roll down the window," he said. "I want to talk to you."

I inched the window down, just a little bit. A seriously bad decision. Talking, as it turned out, was the last thing on Michael's mind. Instead, he reached inside, ripped out the window, and unlocked the door. He jerked it open, grabbed me around the waist, and threw me to the pavement.

I looked up in time to see Michael tearing away in my Firebird, while my mother followed, driving his car.

I got to my feet and stared after them. "Motherfuckers!"

I could hardly believe it. They'd taken all my stuff. My car. My purse. My suitcases and bags. Everything.

This was in the days before cell phones, of course, so I went into the gas station, begged a quarter from the cashier, and called my friend Gaby. I asked her if she could come get me, if I could spend the night with her and her folks, and, thankfully, she said yes.

I'd like to say this was an isolated incident. It would be wonderful to tell you that I had a stable, happy childhood, with few ordeals beyond the typical family bickering, friend drama, and teenage angst.

It would be great to tell you that—except it's not true. The day I was abandoned by my crack-addicted mother at an interstate exit wasn't the beginning of my troubles. Nor was it the end of them. I didn't just attend the School of Hard Knocks, I was the frickin' valedictorian of the place.

This is my story. I share it because it's a story of strength, survival, and, ultimately, optimism.

I'll turn 50 soon. When I look back over the years, all I can say is, "God must think I'm a badass, to put me through all this and expect me to keep on smiling."

But I *do* keep smiling—and you can, too, no matter what your life looks like today.

If things look bad for you right now, please know you're not alone, and know that the tough times won't last forever. Conversely, if things look good, know that the more you learn, the more aware you are, the better you'll be able to handle the inevitable ups and downs.

I wrote this book to share my journey from trauma, fear, and grief to mental wellness, as well as to provide you with inspiration as you take steps on your own journey, regardless of where you are today.

I've learned how to stop asking the question, "Why is this happening to me?" Now, when unexpected things happen, I ask myself, "What am I learning from this? What is this teaching me?"

One thing I know for sure: I was not put on this earth to go through as much crazy stuff as I have, only to sit on a floor and cry. I'm meant to learn, share, empower, and inspire.

I'm a badass—and you are, too. If you ever doubt your badassery, remember this: you're human. Being human means you've been through good times and bad. You've found your way through the bad times, knowing the good ones would come again.

And that's the most badass thing anyone can do.

HOW TO READ THIS BOOK

As I mentioned, I wrote this book both to share and to inspire. In general, the following chapters are divided into the time periods of my life. And yeah, some of those times have been better than others!

I suggest you start at the beginning and read the book through. But, depending on your stage of life, you may find some chapters resonate for you more than others. True to Myself is meant to be a reference; you can pick up this book again and again, anytime you need inspiration.

At the end of each chapter, you'll find a series of questions, titled "Ask Yourself..." I encourage you to think about the scenarios presented through the questions, and ask yourself what you would do in those situations. This exercise is intended to help you be true to yourself when and if you face similar circumstances.

Be thoughtful and introspective, but have fun, too! We're all in this to learn—together.

CHAPTER 2

HERE FOR A REASON

CROOKED BRANCHES ON OUR FAMILY TREE

My history, like everyone else's, starts with my family tree. I know little about my biological father's family, but on my mother's side, I know plenty.

Irv and Ruth Lane were my mom's parents. They were both married to other people when they met. Irv had a daughter with his first wife. Ruth and her first husband had two kids. Eventually, Ruth and Irv ran off together to Reno—that's what you had to do in the 1940s, if you wanted a quickie divorce—and married each other. They left their exes and the children from their first marriages. They never saw those kids again.

I don't know how they could just abandon their kids like that, but they did. Ruth and Irv pretended their pasts didn't exist, and they went on to have three children together. Their eldest was my mother, Harriet. (She later changed her name to Michelle; for simplicity's sake, I call her Michelle throughout this book.) She was followed by my uncle, Richard, and my aunt, Nancy. They lived in Baltimore.

Growing up, Michelle, Richard, and Nancy were super close. Eventually, Richard moved to New Orleans. When I was a kid, we didn't see him much, but Nancy was always around. Michelle was five years older than Nancy, and when they were kids, Nancy worshipped her big sister.

No one in the family, not even my grandmother, knew exactly what my grandfather did for a living. He had a station wagon with the name of a painting company printed on the side, but that was a front; no one ever saw him so much as pick up a paintbrush. It was pretty clear that he was a con man of some sort. He had plenty of money. But back then, no one knew that, either, because he was so stingy about spending it.

My grandmother was under her husband's thumb. She was emotionally unstable, yet she always looked gorgeous. On my grandmother's side of the family, everyone was always having breakdowns, but they had to have their lashes on.

FIFTY WAYS TO LEAVE YOUR LOVER (AND MEET A NEW ONE)

My dad's name was Barry. He and my mother married young, and had their first child, my brother, Andy, in 1965 when Michelle was just 19.

Not long afterward, the entire family—my grandparents, my parents, Andy, and Nancy—moved to Miami, because my grandparents wanted to retire there. The family lived in North Miami Beach. In May of 1970, I was born at North Miami General Hospital.

As a kid, I never knew Barry. My brother had a bit of a relationship with him, but I never did. That's because when I was four months old, Barry did the classic, cliché thing: he said he was going out for a pack of cigarettes, and he never came back.

I swear, you can't make this stuff up.

When Barry left, we moved in with my grandparents. Honestly, other than having to move in with her parents, I don't think my mother missed Barry much. In the pockets of clothes he left behind, she found receipts for flowers he'd never given her, restaurant meals he'd never taken her to. Clearly, there was someone else in his life.

Barry's abandonment left us dependent on my grandparents. All those people in one apartment was a tight fit; in fact, they never got me a crib. I had to sleep in one of those playpens people used to keep in their living rooms, somewhere to safely stash the baby while they were busy doing chores or whatever. But normal people also had a nice nursery for their babies, with a comfy crib, a rocking chair, and a changing table.

We were not normal people.

I guess sometimes they forgot to safely stash me, because when I was sixteen months old, I got my hands on a bottle of Valium and ate the entire thing. Luckily, they rushed me to the emergency room and had my stomach pumped.

I was fine, but that was the last straw for my grandmother. She said to my mother, "You gotta find a man to take care of you and these kids. You gotta get out of here. I cannot have you here anymore."

Michelle had no trouble meeting men. She was very beautiful. Even now—she'll be 75 soon—my mother looks gorgeous. She's never been Botoxed, never had anything done. She's always been a natural beauty.

But she had issues. She was unstable; she was suicidal. And she had Obsessive-Compulsive Disorder (OCD). She loved to cook, and she made us a lot of homemade meals and treats, but as a young girl, I was not allowed to cook or bake cakes, because it messed up her kitchen. My mom would walk into a room, and if some object was sitting on the table, she would move it an inch because she didn't like where it was. When I made my bed in the morning, she redid it, because it had to be perfect.

My grandparents didn't know what to do with her. They encouraged her to use her looks to her advantage. Only recently have I learned that when she was in high school, she'd been accepted into the University of Florida School of Journalism, but my grandparents vetoed that idea. They just wanted her to be married.

Over the years, she's been married six times. She was able to get pretty much any guy she wanted, but she had such a negative view of herself, she didn't think she deserved anyone except losers.

I was two when she hooked up with Husband Number Two. His name was Stanley Michaelson, and he was a cabana manager for pools.

My grandmother said, "Does he have a house?"

"Uh huh," my mom replied.

"Is he married?"

"No."

"Good," my grandmother said. "Go marry him. Get out."

TREASURED TIMES

Stanley Michaelson adored my mother, but Andy and I were like the gift with purchase. Nonetheless, he adopted us.

The years of happiness I recall from my childhood were between the ages of five and eight. Stanley sold his house and rented us a condo in a building called Treasure House. It was a great place to live. There were tons of families; I made a lot of friends. In my memories of those times, everybody was laughing. It was Miami, it was the disco years, and everyone was having fun.

Not only that, but that period represented the first and only stability of my childhood. All the families in the building were so close. I felt like I had multiple moms, dads, and siblings among the families living there. I started school, and I loved it because I was in class with all my friends.

Then one day after school, I was playing at a friend's apartment. My friend's mom came into her room and told me, "Marni, your mother called. You need to go home right away. Your father has left your family; he's disappeared."

I went home and was informed that Stanley was gone, we had nothing, and we had to move out of Treasure House immediately.

Years later, I found out what really happened: my mother and Stanley were involved in insurance fraud. They helped people report their necklaces and rings as stolen, then took a cut of the insurance money. But somebody saw a picture of Stanley wearing a "stolen" necklace at my brother's bar mitzvah. They confronted my mother and Stanley, then went to the police.

The whole thing had been my mother's idea, but Stanley took the rap for her. He went to jail and lost everything. Everything.

She didn't want to say to me, "Your father was arrested because we did insurance fraud." So at that point, I didn't know. She led me to believe that Stanley had abandoned us.

I had to leave the apartment I loved, and move with my mom and Andy into a one-bedroom garden apartment near my grandparents' place. Andy and I had the bedroom, and our mom slept on the couch.

FANCY SCHMANCY

Around this time, Aunt Nancy, with whom I'd always been very close, married her second husband, Jerry Blair. Before that, she'd been married to another guy, Elliott, and they had a son, my cousin Ross. But things didn't work out with Elliott. When Nancy met Jerry, she fell head over heels for him.

Nancy had always been glamorous. I idealized her for it. Her closet was stuffed with fancy clothes; I was in awe. She'd always been that way, but her life with Uncle Jerry took it to another level. He took her into a world of cocaine, partying, and opulence.

Looking back now, I'd say their wedding, in 1978, was the beginning of the bad times. I didn't recognize my aunt anymore. Instead of being a role model who loved me and whom I could look up to, Nancy became a different person, more interested in appearances and what other people thought than she was in her family.

She became Fancy Schmancy Aunt Nancy.

To make matters worse, Jerry had three kids of his own: two sons and a daughter, Lisa, who was a couple of years younger than me. Lisa and I were flower girls in Nancy and Jerry's wedding. I was so young, but I vividly remember Lisa's resentment that I was even *in* the wedding. Lisa had two brothers and a stepbrother; she didn't want another girl around, vying for her stepmother's attention.

So now Nancy had this whole new family that included another little girl, but didn't include me. I kept it inside, but it destroyed me.

My mother, Andy, and I lived in that one-bedroom place for the next few years. I did okay; I liked school and made some friends. Still, when I look at pictures from that time, I see sadness in my eyes. I lost the sparkle I'd had before. They say the eyes are windows to the soul, and I believe that's true.

Those years were hard on Andy, too. He was a teenager, and he had no male role model in his life.

He got a job at a place called the Sea Shanty, and he was so proud to be working. He bought a little moped and rode that to and from work. One night, they gave him a live lobster to take home for dinner. He was so excited, he started to cook the lobster as soon as he got home.

My mother had been out, and she came home to find somebody in her kitchen. She picked up the pot of boiling water with the lobster in it and hurled it across the room. Then she started beating Andy with a broom. He was bigger than her, so he was able to grab the broom. He smashed it and threw it at our mom.

I stood there witnessing this, thinking how crazy it was. Within seconds, her rage went from zero to a hundred percent. There she was, trying to beat the crap out of my brother…for the crime of cooking a lobster in her kitchen.

At the time, I had little sympathy for her. But over the years, I've learned to see it a bit differently. Without a doubt, there's no excuse to hurt your child, the way she was hurting Andy—but after becoming a parent myself, and knowing how feelings of frustration about certain situations can overcome you, I better understand why she wanted to lash out.

I understand the urge, but I wish she hadn't done that. I wish that instead of reacting in that way, she'd sought the professional mental health services she clearly needed.

But people rarely did that, in those days.

MY NAME IS MILTON, AND I'M A MAFIOSO

During this period, my mother, Michelle, met a guy named Milton. She was at the Dallas airport, changing planes. I think they met in the airport bar or something.

For Milton, it was love at first sight. He was older than Michelle and thought he'd hit the jackpot, having someone that young and beautiful interested in him. Milton would have done anything for my mom—and she knew it.

Milton had a lot of money. He was involved in the Jewish Mafia. He never lived in Miami, but he frequently came to visit us, and he started to take my mother and me on a lot of trips, especially to Las Vegas. Andy rarely joined us; he was working, and he stayed home by himself.

Vegas was a whole new world for me, a world of celebrities, bookies, and booze. I felt pretty sophisticated, living that lifestyle. Milton paid for fancy hotel rooms for Michelle and me. I can remember seeing Cher perform. I remember a dinner party hosted by Steve Wynn. Diana Ross was the honoree.

Recently, my mother showed me a picture of her and Barry Gibb from a New Year's Eve party. She also went out with Ralph Renick, who was an icon in Miami; he was the anchorman on Channel 4 News for decades. He'd send limos to pick us up and take us on his boat. He even attended Passover at my grandmother's place one year.

My mother was dating Milton—and she was happy to accept cash, gifts, and perks from him—but that didn't mean he was the only man who got her attention.

In 1980, at the end of fourth grade, I went to sleepaway camp in North Carolina for the summer. I had a great time, except when my mother didn't show up for Parents' Visiting Day. I remember feeling so sad and lonely, seeing all the other kids with their parents.

On the final day of camp, the staff told me, "Marni, your mother's not coming to pick you up. She just got remarried, and you're moving to Vegas."

All of the kids at camp were from Miami, and we'd flown to Asheville together on a charter flight. We were supposed to do the same thing for the return trip; our parents would meet us at the Miami airport.

But it didn't work out that way for me. I went with the group to the airport, but I didn't get on the chartered flight. I don't know the exact details, but I guess my mom booked me a flight to Vegas, and she told the camp people, "She's not getting on the charter back to Miami. Just get her to the terminal and send her off to Vegas."

That experience still resonates with me. I remember all the kids being so excited to go back to Miami. All the chatter on the bus and at the airport. Then they all got on their chartered plane and were gone. I went on a separate flight by myself, to Vegas.

I figured my mother had married Milton, but I was wrong. She'd met some guy named Jay while I was away at summer camp, and he lived in Vegas, so that's

They say
abandonment is a
wound that never
heals.
I say only that an
abandoned child
never forgets.

- Mario Balotelli

where we would live now, too. I never went back to our one-bedroom place in Miami. I didn't get to say goodbye to my friends.

It turned out that my mother and Jay were running a bookie gambling/escort service. There were specific phones for the service in our apartment, and Andy and I were forbidden from touching those phones.

Not that it mattered, because we weren't in Vegas for very long, only two months. In October, we moved to Philadelphia.

I actually really liked Philadelphia. We lived in a suburb called Huntingdon Valley. My mother and Jay opened a deli/restaurant in another suburb nearby, called Jenkintown. I made new friends. I was always good at making friends, an advantage for a girl who moved as often as I did!

We had a decent-sized house in a family neighborhood, even if it was the only house in the neighborhood with no landscaping. People probably figured there was something kind of fishy going on, and if so, it's possible that they weren't far off base.

I didn't have a relationship with Jay, my stepfather. But it was okay. He was a chef and went about his business. My mom helped him in the restaurant, and Andy and I went to school and had relatively normal lives.

It lasted less than a year.

The next summer, 1981, I returned to camp. Again, it was great, but at the end, it was sort of the opposite experience of the year before: instead of flying back to Philly, I was put on the charter flight to Miami with all the other campers.

It turned out that Jay was gone. I mean that literally. It was just "bye-bye, Jay"—he'd vanished.

I still don't know what Jay did to my mother, but whatever

happened, it was bad enough that Michelle called on Milton, her Jewish Mafia boyfriend, to help out. And "help out" he did: Milton had some thugs brutally beat Jay.

And the restaurant? Gone. Blown up.

We never saw Jay again.

Mafia Milton was Michelle's sugar daddy. He was much older than her, and there were so many things about him she couldn't stand. The way he walked. How he'd ask for coffee in the middle of the afternoon. She'd say, "I'm not messing up my kitchen at this time of the day."

We were back in Miami, living in an apartment that Milton paid for. We had no idea where our stepfather, Jay, had gone. No one seemed to know if he'd been in the restaurant when it exploded. I still don't know. It was never talked about afterward.

Looking back now, it seems crazy that my mother expected Andy and me to go through all of this and not be affected. People think kids are so resilient. That's true, but it doesn't mean there's no long-term effect.

I was surviving, I was making friends, but it was not a typical childhood. There was no such thing as "normal" in my life.

During this time, Nancy and Jerry lived nearby, in a condo complex called the Jockey Club. We would meet them to go out for dinner. First, you'd have to meet at the bar, the club, then we'd go eat. It was always, "Meet us at the club."

On Sundays, we spent all day at the Jockey Club's pool, then later we'd meet back at the bar. There was flair, a bookie, and lots of booze. It wasn't neighborhood barbecues on Sundays. Not in my world.

By this time, Andy was 17, and he was mostly staying with

Stanley. Although Stanley had lost everything when he went to jail, he was out now, and he had a little house behind someone else's house. He was living a modest lifestyle, and he wanted nothing to do with my mother, but he did let Andy stay with him. Andy and I were never close, so I can't really say what was going on with him—whether he was happy, whether he was content. When he graduated from high school, he went into the Navy. He wanted to get away, I guess, and I couldn't blame him.

One day, my mother told me she ran into Ronny, her high school boyfriend. They started dating and got married. He had three children, and I was pretty excited. *Finally*, I thought, *I'll have siblings to hang out with!*

My elation was short-lived. About a year later, Ronny was caught stealing and went to jail. My mother divorced him, and I never saw my step-siblings again.

I hoped for some stability from Fancy Schmancy Aunt Nancy and her family, but that was hit-or-miss. On weekends, they had Jerry's three kids and Ross, Aunt Nancy's kid. Often, they'd take the kids to do something fun—an amusement park, shopping, the beach—and sometimes I was included, as if I were part of the family. But other weekends, I was not invited to join them. There was no rhyme or reason to it; whether I was included or not was entirely dependent on Jerry's moods. He ruled everything in their house; my involvement with them was no exception.

CAN'T WE JUST BE BORING, FOR A CHANGE?

In those years, my mother and I were the clichéd single mom with a daughter. I craved normalcy, and looking back, I can see that's the reason I fought like a motherfucker to get the house where my daughter, Taylor, grew up. I wanted Taylor, who's now 19, to have the most boring, stable, suburban childhood possible. I never had a real childhood, so I've relived childhood through Taylor. (More on that later.)

I wish my mother—or someone—would have said to me, when I was a child, "Let me take you to talk to somebody. I know it's been a lot, all of these changes." Instead, it was, "Accept it. What are you upset about? You have somewhere to live, what more do you want?"

DON'T LET ANYONE DULL YOUR SPARKLE!

My heart breaks for my younger self. If I knew a girl right now going through what I went through back then—oh, my God, I wouldn't leave that girl's side.

She would be so loved. She would know she could do anything in this world.

ASK YOURSELF...

- Which memories from childhood are most painful for you? Which make you the happiest?
- What can childhood pain teach you about your own resilience and strength?
- If you have children (or would like to someday), in what ways does/will your parenting differ from how you were raised? Conversely, are there aspects of your childhood that you would like to recreate for your own children?

CHAPTER 3

NEVER, EVER GIVE UP

LIVING TO PLEASE

When I was a teenager, I lived my life to please Fancy Schmancy Aunt Nancy. My mother was in her own little world, and by the time I was in my late teens, she was on crack. So Aunt Nancy, by default, became my more "stable" mother figure.

But there was a catch. Aunt Nancy only loved me if I was thin, if I said the right things, if I acted the right way. Otherwise, she wanted nothing to do with me.

Nancy's husband, Jerry, was just a bully, and his daughter Lisa was insanely jealous of me. Honestly, she was a kid with a lot of problems, and she wasn't well liked by her peers. I remember her bat mitzvah—not one friend showed up. If you've ever been to a bar or bat mitzvah, you know that would be devastating for a teen.

I didn't have a bat mitzvah or attend Hebrew school. In my world, those things were mostly for boys. My mom loved parties; if we *had* been religious, I'm sure she would have thrown something fabulous for me. The only reason Lisa had a bat mitzvah was because Jerry wanted to show off his wealth.

But I had something Lisa never had: friends. I always had friends, despite all the moving around we did. When I turned 13, I had a joint birthday party with my friend Tara.

I have some pictures from that party. Looking at them now, you can see how pretty my mother was, and how I took after her. But I had no idea, at the time, that I was pretty. No one ever complimented my looks. Instead, I agonized over every aspect of my appearance.

FRIENDS, SCHOOL, AND ACCEPTANCE

Despite having a lot of various friends, I didn't have a bestie. I remember at camp when I was 13, it was a "free choice" day. You could do whatever you wanted, but I didn't have anyone to do anything with. I remember sitting on a big rock by myself, thinking maybe I wasn't worthy of having a best friend. In retrospect, I wonder if it was a matter of "worthiness" or if I was just afraid to get super close to anyone. If I completely trusted another person, what would I do if she abandoned me, as so many already had?

I wish my mother had said, "Maybe there's a therapist you could talk to. Let's look into it." But no, things like that were taboo. Probably not just for me, either; it was pretty unusual for kids to see therapists back then. We were expected to just deal with any troubles we were having in life.

As for school, neither Aunt Nancy nor my mother cared about my grades. My mother told me it was fine if I got Ds. I don't think anyone believed I was intelligent enough to pull better than a D in any subject, and as a result, I didn't think I was, either.

How I looked was much more important than how I did in school. Every Monday morning, I was weighed. I had to be pretty; I had to be thin.

When I was 16, my mother insisted I get my nose done. It was a rite of passage; every sixteen-year-old girl where I came from did that. When it was finished, my mother studied it from every angle. Even on crack, she did that.

She said to the plastic surgeon, "There's a little bit…right there…" She insisted I have my nose done a second time, because it wasn't flawless the first time around. While the surgeon was at it, she had him give me a chin implant, because my chin had to be perfect for my profile.

It was the opposite when my daughter, Taylor, was that age. The main thing I cared about was that she got good grades, so she could go to college. I always praised her highly for doing well in school.

That being said, I admit that I *almost* got caught up in the "how you look" stuff when Taylor was a teen. I remember one day she came down the stairs, and I didn't like what she was wearing. There was nothing wrong with her outfit; I just didn't find it flattering. I said, "Uh, uh—go upstairs and change."

Afterward, I realized I was starting to define her by her weight, not by the good girl she was. *I'm becoming my mother*, I thought. And I refused to let that happen. I started seeing a therapist, because I knew I needed help in my relationship with my daughter. And I never spoke that way to Taylor again.

MAFIA MILTON TO THE RESCUE (AGAIN)

During these years, Mafia Milton was paying my mother's bills. He paid for my plastic surgery and for our home in Miami, a swanky condo in a building called The Hamptons.

He also still took my mother and me on a lot of trips. He'd say to my mother, "I'm going to Atlantic City; I want you to come along." Because of his Mafia involvement, he traveled with an alias. He was always in the casino; that's why we'd get comped for our accommodations.

I can remember being 14, sitting in a magnificent suite at the Golden Nugget, complete with butlers. In our condo in Miami, my mother had a phone installed in my bathroom, so when I was doing my makeup, I could make calls if I wanted to.

She'd take me to get my nails done, and I've had them done pretty much ever since. A manicure is like a part of my fingers now. I don't know what my hands would feel like if they weren't manicured.

Even when my mother got married to other guys, Milton was still in her life. He begged her to marry him, but she refused. She said he was too old and ugly to be her husband.

Without a doubt, she used him, but I think it was because she never felt worthy. She could have gone out with affluent, sophisticated men. But she felt like such garbage, she only went with garbage.

At the time, I had no idea what crack was, much less that my mother was on it. I was so naïve, when someone at school told me about crack, I just thought you put cocaine in a joint, rolled it up, and smoked it. I had no idea what my mother was really doing. I was blind to what she was really like, in her drug-infused world.

But people don't ask to be born the way they are. When she was young, the people in my mother's life enabled it. They just let her be. Nobody thought to get her help for her mental issues.

My grandmother was tough on my mother, but with my

grandfather, who controlled the purse strings, she was meek. She wasn't capable of helping my mother in any way, and my grandfather was not interested in doing that.

GROWING UP...TOO FAST

In eighth grade, I lost my virginity. The boy told me he loved me. Afterward, he broke up with me. To say I was devastated would be the understatement of the year.

Looking back, I don't think girls who have a good self-image—especially girls who have a great father or another stable male role model in their lives—generally make that type of (poor) choice at such a young age. But it wasn't unusual for girls like me to do that. It still isn't unusual.

These days, when I talk with teen girls, often they say, "The pressure gets to me. I feel like I have to be perfect at everything."

I tell them, "You're competing with what you *think* you see. You're competing with social media. Don't do that. Be true to who you are."

If you're a girl of this age and you're not feeling great about some aspect of your life, I beg you: find someone to talk to.

"You will be too much for some people. Those aren't your people."
- Glennon Doyle Melton

Ask your parents for help. If that's not an option, ask the guidance counselor at school. Or call a hotline. (A list of resources is at the back of this book.)

There are adults out there who want to help you. When I was a teen, there were so few resources. Now there are a lot. Please, please, make use of them.

"161 WAYS TO DESCRIBE MARNI M"

After I lost my virginity, people looked at me differently. Everybody knew I'd lost my virginity, and I now had a reputation.

The first couple of years of high school, I didn't date much. I think I probably would not have made a great girlfriend anyway, because at that age, I had no idea who I was. I kept trying to change myself, in an effort to fit in.

One afternoon when I was a sophomore, I went upstairs to my locker to get my things and head home. It was the start of winter break, and I was excited, because I was leaving that night to go to New York with a friend and her mom.

As I approached my locker, I stopped in my tracks. There were a ton of kids in the hallway, and there were small pieces of colored paper all over the floor. It reminded me of "color war" at camp, where they divide kids into teams and do all kinds of Olympic-style events. When they break out color war, it's a big festival to learn what team you're on. They throw hundreds of different-colored papers, and you grab one to determine your team.

It looked like that—but it wasn't like that. Everyone was picking up those pieces of paper and reading them with fascination. As I got closer, I saw what the papers said. Each one, on the top, said, "161 Ways to Describe Marni M."

And then it said something about me. Nothing flattering, either. It was one hundred and sixty-one insults, all directed at me.

I learned later that some boy I barely knew had come up with the idea. He wrote most of the insults, with help from a few other people. Then they threw the papers everywhere.

It's funny (well, not really *funny*) to think about that now. Not long ago, I sent a video I'd made on the subject of bullying to the guy who did that to me in high school. I wanted him to know that it still affected me.

To my surprise, he got back in touch with me. And he was the most humble, apologetic guy. He has daughters now; he gets it.

"How could I have done that?" he asked me. "It's unimaginable—when you look at your sixteen-year-old self. Listening to your video, hearing what you went through, Marni, and knowing I did that to you. I am so sorry."

What's interesting is that now, over thirty years later, he couldn't even remember why he'd done it. I guess kids just do stupid things. At the time, it probably sounded funny. He was probably hanging out with his friends, and someone randomly suggested, "Hey, let's pick on somebody." And the somebody turned out to be me.

I forgave him, and he's now one of the sweetest supporters I have. But it goes to show that our actions, both positive and negative, have a long, long reach.

On that afternoon in February of 1986, I didn't know who had done it. I had to go to the principal's office and tell them my side of the story. There wasn't much to tell; I'd had no idea anyone disliked me that much. And even if I'd had suspicions about who started it, I probably wouldn't have said so—because nobody likes a rat, right?

At home, I was in shock. I felt worthless and disgusted with myself. If someone could come up with one hundred and sixty-one terrible things to say about me, I thought, then I must be an awful person.

I'd guess it was the equivalent to what happens to some kids today via social media. It was the 1980s version of cyberbullying.

I remember telling my mother what happened, but I don't remember her reaction to it. As it turned out, maybe she *did* react, in her own way. Much later, I'd learn that was the exact night my mother first tried crack. So maybe that was her way of dealing—or *not* dealing—with her daughter being a social pariah.

In any case, I tried to put it out of my head, instead thinking about flying to New York that night with my friend Rachel and her mom. The trip was just what I needed; Rachel and I really had the best time.

It was a great trip, but afterward, I wished I could go into a shell. I just wanted to hide, you know?

I was telling the "161 Ways" story to someone recently, and they said, "If you could go back and do anything different regarding this situation, what would you do?"

I thought about it, then said, "I would have gone to the school counselor. I would have asked for help from someone, help processing what happened."

The problem, back then, was that when something like that happened, kids would think, "Uh—am I gonna tell the dean, or the principal, or a teacher? No, because I don't want to rat someone out." So most kids who were bullied, like me, didn't say anything.

But if it happened today, I'd make use of the resources available. I'd call a hotline, or look online for help. These days, lots of resources are anonymous. Instead of having to go to your parents or some adult at school (like I would have had to), you can reach out online or on the phone. (Again, please see the appendix for more information.)

If you're the victim of something like this, you might feel worthless. You might want to hide. You might feel like you're the only person in the world experiencing loneliness or bullying.

Social media would have you believe that, because on social media, everyone is always putting their best foot forward. When people post about themselves, it's mostly pictures of good times, happiness, friends.

"Trust yourself.
You've survived a lot,
and you'll survive
whatever is coming."
- Robert Tew

But people feel left out all the time. So many people of every age feel that, in one sense or another, they're not "good enough."

If that's infecting you in any way, please reach out. Please talk to someone about it.

NO SENSE IN HIDING

After the New York trip, I knew I had to face school. I wanted to hide, but I didn't.

Instead, I decided to take action to change my life. There was a boy I kind of liked, named Richard. So I wrote him a note. I think I said something incredibly clever and creative, like,

"You're really cute." But it worked; he ended up asking me on a date.

He became my everything. I dated Richard for about a year. Then I met somebody else, and I forgot about Richard. Too bad! I think I let a good one go. He went on to become an attorney. I saw him some years ago, and I could tell he was a good, sweet man.

In high school, Richard's brother was popular, a football player. I ran into him recently, and I said, "Hey, great to see you! It's Marni, from high school."

He replied, "Oh, in high school you were like 'eww.' But now you look okay."

Geez, I guess you never can tell, right? Even within the same family.

It was such a different world when I was younger. There was nobody for me to have open communication with, no one I could ask for advice. My locker was a mess. I wasn't doing homework. My grades were terrible, but nobody cared. Education was never a priority. No one in my family mentioned the idea of me taking the SAT, or going to college.

UNDER THEIR THUMBS

In all this time, the one constant was Uncle Jerry and Fancy Schmancy Aunt Nancy. I don't mean that they were a constant, nurturing presence. I mean that the world revolved around them. My entire family would do anything for them. If Nancy and Jerry were not talking to you, the minions wouldn't, either. This was because Jerry made so much money. His business was fueling airplanes, and he was very successful. They say money talks, and that sure was true in my family.

Jerry would say, "I'm not a good father. But I'm a great provider." He would rent The Palm Restaurant for the Super Bowl, and we'd all go. Great, right? Except that he loved to invite people he didn't really like, then tell them, "You know what? Get out." It was an ego trip for him.

Because of our mother, our circumstances, Nancy always felt sorry for my brother, Andy. She would give her credit card to him, and if he spent a lot of her (well, Jerry's) money, that was okay.

But she wouldn't do that for me. My existence bothered both Nancy and Jerry.

GYPSY

By the winter of my junior year of high school, my mother had been on crack for a year, but I had no idea. People were coming in our condo in the middle of the night; I would hear the microwave and wonder what they were cooking at 3:00 AM. All my mom would say is that they were her friends.

The one day, one of her "friends" called and spoke to me. She said, "Marni, I'm admitting myself to Mount Sinai Drug Rehab. And I think your mother should do the same. She has a severe problem. You need to get her help."

But I was 16. I had no idea how to do that. After that phone call, I paid more attention to what my mother was doing, and I could see that her friend was right; she was on drugs. But I felt powerless to do anything about it.

One night, the police barged in. Someone had ratted out Michelle and her druggie pals. She threw all her paraphernalia out the window. She was still very glamorous; she didn't look like an addict. She told the police, "I'm just a mom. It was a mistake." And they believed her.

But eventually, the jig was up. Mafia Milton had been footing the bill for our condo, but he became suspicious, and he paid the security people to see who was coming and going at all hours. When Milton found out the truth, he said, "If you're on drugs, Michelle, you're out. I'm not paying for you anymore."

After the incident at the gas station off I-95 (which I talked about in Chapter 1), I stayed with Gaby for a few nights, and then I found another place for a few nights. I became a gypsy; I moved from friend's house to friend's house. None of these people were besties or family friends; they were just girls I knew from school who felt kind of sorry for me.

Their parents would let me stay a week or two, but eventually the parents said, "Enough, Marni—you have to leave." It was too much, having me at their houses.

I began to skip school. I just didn't see the point in going.

Aunt Nancy and Uncle Jerry were no help. They wanted nothing to do with me. And my Uncle Richard, who lived in New Orleans and had no children (and, as an aside, who worked for Uncle Jerry) certainly didn't want me, either.

SITTING SHIVA

Around this same time, my grandmother's health was declining, and I began to visit my grandparents daily. Eventually, my grandfather moved my grandmother into a piece-of-shit nursing home. He said it was all he could afford.

My grandmother passed away in May, the same week, coincidentally, that Mafia Milton threw my mother and me out of the condo at The Hamptons.

A few days before my grandmother's funeral was the night when my mom and her boyfriend stole my car. Despite this, my mom showed up at the funeral, whacked out of her mind. We all tried to ignore her.

After the funeral, they put my grandmother in a crypt. I took a tube of lipstick out of my purse and used it to write, on the outside of the crypt, "I love you." I wrote it as an eye, a heart, and a U. Believe it or not, it's still there, more than thirty years later.

But my family was furious. Uncle Richard and Aunt Nancy didn't see love; they saw this gesture as me being disrespectful, defacing my grandmother's crypt. They thought I did it to be a bitch.

That wasn't it at all. I was grieving—*everything*! My grandmother's death, of course, but also the loss of the slight semblance of stability I'd had, living in The Hamptons with my mother. I was in a state of shock that her drug addiction was so powerful, she chose her crackhead boyfriend over her own daughter.

As a result, I was not permitted to go in the limousine with the rest of the family back to the house. I had to get there on my own.

They let me into the shiva, which was being held at Aunt Nancy and Uncle Jerry's place. (In Jewish tradition when someone dies, the shiva is when their family gathers at home to mourn and greet extended family and friends who want to pay respects.)

I hadn't been at the shiva long when Lisa said to Uncle Jerry, "Marni's being rude to me."

What? I hadn't said a word to Lisa. But I guess she didn't like the way I was looking at her or something.

"Get out," Uncle Jerry told me. "If you can't be nice to Lisa, get out."

"But I have nowhere to go," I told him.

"I don't care," he said. "Get out."

And that was that. They threw me out of my own grandmother's shiva.

LIVING WITH POP

That fall should have been the start of my senior year of high school, but I never really went to twelfth grade. I showed up the day they were taking yearbook pictures, but that was about it.

By then, I'd moved in with my grandfather. He was still living in the apartment they'd moved to when they relocated from Baltimore to Miami, all those years ago. I was with Pop from September until the end of November. I wasn't doing much, just hanging around.

My mother wasn't doing much, either, except crack, of course. During this time, Uncle Jerry said to her, "Michelle, if you get a job, I'll pay you three times the amount the job pays. I just want you to work—doing anything. I don't want you to sit around, expecting people to give you handouts."

But she had no intention of getting a job. I guess it's hard to work when your entire existence is focused on getting your next hit.

Instead, she dug into funds my grandfather had given her. It turned out that, over the years, he'd made Michelle the only other signatory, besides himself, on close to half a million dollars in CDs, or certificates of deposit (basically, timed deposits you can make at a bank or credit union). So much for the "poverty" he'd claimed when he put his wife in a crappy nursing home!

No one could touch that money except Pop and my mother. When she became addicted to crack—and Milton was no longer paying her bills—she cashed in those CDs to pay for her addiction.

Eventually, I don't know how, my grandfather learned what she was doing. I was there, at his place, the day he found out. He started hitting my mother. I don't mean just light punches; he was beating the crap out of her, and she was hitting him right back.

I called Aunt Nancy. "I need your help. Pop and my mother are beating each other up."

Nancy was annoyed, because she had to drive up from North Miami. When she got there, she asked what was going on.

"She stole my money!" Pop screamed.

"What money?" Aunt Nancy asked.

"CDs. Hundreds of thousands in CDs. She was the only other signatory on them, and she's been cashing them in."

"What the *hell*?" Aunt Nancy yelled. "You had that much in CDs, and you let her be a signatory but not me? You let Mom rot away in that schlocky place, when you could have hired a private nurse? You *bastard*!"

Then Nancy started beating my grandfather. Now all three of them were hitting each other.

I just stood there, speechless.

My grandfather was a very selfish man. Before she got sick and died, my grandmother had driven a piece-of-shit car, while he had a Cadillac. She'd eat some cheap cut of meat and he'd have a filet. She catered to him, and when she was gone, his world fell apart.

And now there was a teenager living with him, messing up his living room, disrupting his routines. I admit that I probably wasn't the most helpful kid to have around. My mother had never let me cook, so I didn't know how to make meals for him. I didn't clean. And since I was no longer going to school, I was basically just *there*—probably driving him nuts.

He couldn't take it. Finally, the day before Thanksgiving, he gathered all my clothes and things. There was a big dumpster behind his building, and he took all my stuff and threw it in.

I called Aunt Nancy. "Pop just threw my clothes away."

She came up to his place, about a twenty-minute drive, and just looked at me, then said, "Thanks for ruining my Thanksgiving."

THE BIG EASY

Nancy told me, "I'm sending you to New Orleans, to live with Andy."

By then, Andy had become a police officer, I think mostly because he wanted to arrest people involved with drugs and beat the crap out of them. Ironically, he also smoked a lot of pot. So, my brother was half police officer, half pothead.

"Can't I live with Uncle Richard instead?" I asked Nancy.

She shrugged. "I doubt it, but you can call him and ask."

But when I called, Uncle Richard said no. "I can't talk to you, Marni, much less let you move in," he said. "I know Nancy's barely speaking to you, so I can't have anything to do with you, either."

That was that. In December 1987, when I was 17, Aunt Nancy sent me to New Orleans. I moved in with Andy.

New Orleans might be nicknamed "the Big Easy," but it was

anything besides easy for me. I went to Grace King High School and I made a few friends, but really, I didn't have much in common with anybody. I guess it was kind of culture shock.

I was pretty lonely. Andy made it clear that he didn't want me there, any more than I wanted to be there.

During this period, thoughts of suicide definitely filtered through my brain. In some ways, it seemed like the easiest solution. But when a thought like that came along, I stuffed it down. I decided this was just how life was supposed to be.

I stayed for a few months, but the whole time, I wanted to get out of there, get away from Andy. So I called a guy named Mark, back in Florida. Before Aunt Nancy shipped me off to New Orleans, I'd been kind of dating Mark, who was a year older than me.

Mark told me he'd see what he could do. He got in touch with Aunt Nancy, who agreed to give him a car and a credit card so he could drive out and get me.

"There's one condition," Nancy told him. "Don't bring her back to me. I don't want anything to do with that girl."

I never graduated from high school. In April of 1988, just shy of my eighteenth birthday, Mark arrived in New Orleans to get me. And we just left.

THE NOT-SO-MAGIC KINGDOM

On the way back to Miami, we stopped in Orlando, where Disney World is. Mark said, "I've decided we're not going back to Miami. We're gonna live here."

I didn't have any say in the matter, but I figured it was better than being in New Orleans, and better than nobody wanting me in Miami. I got a job at a daycare center. Mark worked at a gas station, taking money from the mini-mart and pocketing it.

There was no bed in our place. We slept on the floor.

One of Mark's favorite pastimes was beating the shit out of me. I knew it was wrong, and I was terrified of him. I wanted to leave, but I had nowhere else to go.

After a few months, I said to him, "I want to live in Miami. Please, can we go back to North Miami Beach?"

We moved back and ended up at the apartment building where I'd lived with my mother when I was 12, when she was married to husband number four, Ronny. I couldn't afford my own place, so I moved into that building with Mark.

He got his kicks from doing things like locking me out on the balcony. He was still using me as a human punching bag. And he was cheating on me, of course—what else would you expect?

Finally, I called Aunt Nancy and begged for help. She called the police, and when they got there, they found me huddled in a corner, terrified. They escorted me out and took me to Nancy.

She took me in for the night, but in the morning, she told me I had to get a job and move on.

"Find your own place," she said. "Get a roommate. I'm not taking care of you."

GROWN-UP TEENAGER

Earlier that year, in May, I'd turned 18—a legal adult—but I didn't have the things that I thought adults were supposed to have: a job, a place to live. Again, I was a gypsy, going from house to house, staying with anyone who would take me in for a few days.

Aunt Nancy and Uncle Jerry didn't want to support me, so

they found me a job at a travel agency, through some people they knew who owned that business. I had a few other jobs during that time, too, kind of no-brainer jobs that I found on my own.

Eventually, I was able to scrape together enough money for a security deposit. By the time I turned 19, I had an apartment and a roommate. She was sweet, but not around much. I was doing my best to get by, make a life for myself, but I was really lonely.

I hadn't seen Michelle since my grandmother's shiva. In fact, I didn't talk to my mother from age 17 until I was pregnant with my first child at age 29. (More on that later.)

After Milton tossed Michelle out, I never saw him again except for one time, years later, when I lived for a while in the building next door to The Hamptons. I saw a man on the other side of the pool, and I was pretty sure it was Milton. I recognized the hunched-over way he walked.

I went up to him. "Milton—it's Marni."

He nodded and said hello, but then he walked on. He didn't want anything to do with me.

RESILIENCE

When I recall those times, the word that comes to mind is *resilience*. I didn't give up. I couldn't give up, not if I wanted to survive.

Still, I wish I'd known how to not only survive, but actually thrive. I wish I'd known how to stay true to myself.

When I look back at family history—when I think about how submissive my grandmother was—it's not surprising how both my mother and Aunt Nancy turned out, and how that affected me. My grandmother didn't give her daughters a powerful message of self-worth and acceptance. As a result, Michelle and Nancy both had a lot of problems; they just took it down different avenues. They didn't know how to love themselves, much less love other people. I guess when they told me to lose weight or took

"Don't stop dreaming just because you had a nightmare."
- Jill Scott

me to get my nails done, those things might have been how they gave affection, in a sick way.

Aunt Nancy probably wanted a daughter. She had her son, Ross, who was a mess. And she had her stepdaughter, Lisa, who didn't have much potential. I guess I filled that "daughter" role for Nancy, and yet, she hated how I looked at 14, 15. My frizzy hair, my weight, my teenage awkwardness. She wanted me to be petite, thin, and as stylish as she was. At 15!

It's kind of ridiculous, when you think about it. No one should expect a girl to be glamorous at 15. That's a time in life when you're trying to figure out who you are. The job of the grown-ups around you is to help you navigate those waters, so you can make your way toward a well-adjusted adulthood.

When my own daughter, Taylor, was in high school, I worked hard to break that cycle. I had to consciously work to accept her, even when she dressed in ways that I didn't like. I had to remind myself that as long as Taylor was treating herself and other people well, that was all that mattered.

There have been a few times when Taylor wanted to reach out to Aunt Nancy, wanted to try building some sort of relationship with her. But I said to her, "Do not call Nancy. I do not want you being shushed and thrown out and discarded, like I was."

Sometimes I'll be looking up at the sky, and I'll talk to my grandmother.

"You all thought Andy and Ross were the good kids," I say to her. "They're the fucked-up ones. I was the only normal one… but nobody knew it."

ASK YOURSELF…

- Have you experienced abandonment, abuse, or bullying? If so, what steps can you take to explore your feelings about these experiences?
- Women and girls have a tendency to be hard on each other. Instead, how can we lift each other up?
- If you're not happy with your appearance, could there be reasons that go beyond your looks? Is someone else pressuring you to look a certain way? Are you unhappy, and is this affecting you physically? If so, consider discussing these issues with a loved one and/or a professional.

CHAPTER 4

"JUST FIND A RICH MAN" (*WAIT – WHAT???*)

A PORSCHE AND A BOAT...WHAT MORE DO YOU NEED?

In 1989, I was 19 years old and just floating around Miami. I'd be living with a roommate, then one or the other of us would decide to move, and I'd be living with another roommate. I went from job to job. Nothing was permanent, but at least I was able to pay my bills, as long as I lived frugally.

Then one day, a friend said to me, "I know this guy, Lawrence. He's thirty-four. I realize that's kinda old, but you're very sophisticated. Maybe you can go out with him."

"What's he like?" I asked.

"He has a Porsche 928 S4. And a boat. He owns a law firm."

I shrugged. "Okay. Why not?"

Turned out Lawrence did have all those things: money, his own business, a nice apartment. A hot car and a boat. Problem was, he was god-awful-looking. But I tried to see past it. All my life I'd heard the message, from my mother, from Aunt Nancy, to go out with an older guy, one with money. So, I figured this was my path.

If Lawrence had treated me like a queen, his looks wouldn't have mattered. But he didn't. He'd take me to the mall but wouldn't buy me anything, not even a soda. He'd invite me to glamorous parties he threw for his clients and staff. But he didn't walk me around those parties, introducing me and showing people how much he loved having me as a girlfriend. In fact, he barely noticed I was there.

"Don't complain," my friend Lorie said. "At least you have a boyfriend."

YOUR BEAUTY IS IN BEING YOURSELF

In those days, Lorie was my best friend. She was thin and pretty; she went out with a ton of guys. I was her chubby sidekick.

Nowadays, I'm not a fan of the scale; I'm not even sure of my current weight. But back then, I weighed about 170 pounds. I'm five-foot-three, and I didn't work out in those days, so this was kind of an unhealthy weight for me.

I remember wearing a bikini around Aunt Nancy, who would say something like, "God, I can't look at it." Yes, she'd actually say that—*it*. Like my body was a separate, despicable creature.

My weight truly bothered her. It affected her mood. If I lost a few pounds, she'd be so happy. She'd say, "Look how great Marni looks!"

Aunt Nancy never asked—and I doubt she even wondered—was I happy? Was I healthy?

Was I okay?

"Beauty begins the moment you decide to be yourself."
- Coco Chanel

Recently, I was looking at a photo of myself from that time. It was a picture of nineteen-year-old Marni, trying to be Nancy. I also found a picture of my brother and me when I was in my twenties. When I look at those pictures now, all I can think about is how critical I was of myself. But truly, I was beautiful.

WHAT'S IN A NAME?

On Friday nights, everyone used to go to TGI Fridays. And that's where I met a guy named Dean Shechtman. He was with his cousin, Brian, a guy I knew from the Jockey Club, where Aunt Nancy and Uncle Jerry lived. Brian's parents were friends with my aunt and uncle.

Dean asked me out the night before my twentieth birthday. I was still seeing Lawrence, but I thought Dean was cute. And more importantly, he was *not* Lawrence. Compared to Lawrence, Dean was Prince Charming.

He was three years older than me. We'd gone to the same high school, but we didn't know each other back then. In high school, Dean had been an amazing athlete. He played a variety of sports, but softball was his big thing. They said his arm was like a rocket.

When I heard who he was, I threw myself at Dean. "Oh, you're a Shechtman? That's your family?"

I knew Aunt Nancy would approve. But neither she nor I knew, at the time, that Dean's branch of the family was very different from the Jockey Club Shechtmans. Dean's parents lived in Orlando, in a modest neighborhood.

Even when Aunt Nancy learned that Dean's branch of the family wasn't wealthy, she still asked me, "Does he work? Does he make a good living?"

I shrugged. "Yeah, I guess so."

"Good. Go after him."

That was the only requirement. Could a man take care of you? That was all that mattered.

A RING ON MY FINGER AND A ROOF OVER MY HEAD

With Aunt Nancy's words as my compass, I figured I'd finally made it, being Dean's girlfriend. But I cringe when I think about how he treated me. He threw me out of the bedroom for not having sex with him. If I said I was too tired or not in the mood, he'd say, "Fine, then get out. You can't sleep in my bedroom."

And I actually did it. I slept on his couch.

Dean's job was selling health insurance to the elderly people. In small Florida hick towns, he'd go door-to-door selling insurance policies. He made a great living, so I figured he must be an excellent salesman. Old people sure seemed to love him, and that was a good sign, I thought.

What I didn't know—didn't find out until years later, actually—was that he was selling life insurance, not health insurance, without his clients' knowledge. He would cover the forms with another paper, and they'd sign up for life insurance. His commission on life insurance was almost 99 percent. For health insurance, the commission was very low, but he wasn't making most of his money that way. It was all falsified life insurance policies. It was a scam. But at the time, I didn't know that.

I moved in with Dean in November of that year. I figured it got me out of the merry-go-round of roommates. He didn't charge me rent, so that saved me quite a bit of money.

Also, it got a ring on my finger. I told him, "I'm not gonna move into your apartment unless we get engaged." So we went to the mall and he bought me a little diamond ring.

He didn't want to marry me, and looking back, I have to say he was right to be hesitant. We were both so young, and there was no reason to get married. But I insisted on it, and he agreed.

I didn't marry Dean for love. I married him for a roof over my head. All I'd ever wanted was a house with a pool, in the suburbs. Growing up, I never had that—and I thought if Dean could give me that, then I'd be secure and happy.

We got married in January 1992. The only reason we had a big wedding was because of Fancy Schmancy Aunt Nancy, who told me, "I'm gonna throw you the most fabulous wedding."

And she did. Nancy pulled out all the stops: dress, flowers, an expensive venue for the reception, open bar. I remember thinking, *oh my God, this is breathtaking.*

It was only much later that I realized my wedding was just Aunt Nancy's way of having a big party. It didn't have anything to do with celebrating my marriage. She made me give every dime we got as a wedding gift to her, to offset the wedding expenses.

My uncle, Jerry Blair, hated Dean's uncle, Jerry Shechtman, Brian's dad. Jerry Shechtman owned a huge yacht that was used for parties. My Uncle Jerry had his daughter Lisa's bat mitzvah on that yacht. But Jerry Shechtman loved to control the parties that took place on his yacht. He had as big an ego as my uncle's, and they were always at odds.

At Lisa's bat mitzvah on his yacht, Jerry Shechtman ordered separate food for his table. Chateaubriand steak (which Jerry Blair had ordered for all the guests) was not good enough for Jerry Shechtman, who wanted lobster. That infuriated Jerry

Blair, because Jerry Shechtman was there as a guest, not as an owner.

So when I married Dean, my uncle Jerry Blair's favorite part was when he got to say, "All you Shechtman people, get the fuck out of my party."

I hated that he did that. He was such a bully, my uncle. Inevitably, when he threw a party, including my wedding, he'd get drunk, and somebody would get yelled at and end up leaving the party in tears.

"LIFE IS A GAME… LEARN HOW TO PLAY IT."

Aunt Nancy used to say to me, "Life is a game. You have to learn how to play it. When Jerry's talking, shut your mouth."

Maybe she was right about that "game" business. All I knew was that I wanted to be loved. Every morning, I would call my aunt to say hi. And she would either say, "Marn?" which meant she was happy, or she'd say, "What's doing?"

If she did that, I would get all panicky. "What did I do wrong?"

Generally, I hadn't done *anything* wrong. But it didn't matter. In Nancy's eyes, I didn't do anything right, either. I could tell her that I cured cancer, and she would say, "Well, I'm sure you didn't do it by yourself."

It was different for Lisa. They accepted her the way she was. Even stuff that had nothing to do with me, they turned it into my fault.

Lisa was an awkward, klutzy girl, and I don't know how she did it, but in those days, she was married to an adorable boy named Rick. The month after my wedding, I said to Rick, "What did you get Lisa for Valentine's Day?"

"Nothing."

"You can't go home without chocolate," I told him. "You gotta give her something. Here, take my box of chocolate, give it to Lisa."

That night, Aunt Nancy called me. "How *dare* you have Rick in your home?"

You know, in my world, no good deed went unpunished.

Uncle Jerry liked Dean; they would play tennis together, and Jerry would bet on the games, making sure Dean was on his team. Uncle Jerry's two sons didn't live up to his expectations, but because Dean was into sports, he became the son Jerry had always wanted.

AND BABY WOULD MAKE...*HOW* MANY?

Lisa never had kids. Neither did Aunt Nancy's son, Ross. One of Uncle Jerry's sons has a few kids, but they were never close. So Nancy and Jerry basically had no grandchildren.

But Dean and I weren't providing them with "substitute" grandkids, either. After trying for a while with no luck, we looked into fertility issues. For his part, Dean didn't want to do anything to remedy the situation. So I did it all, IUI, Clomid, the whole bit. I even did in vitro fertilization, which is fairly invasive. I was in my mid-twenties, probably the youngest patient the fertility doc had ever seen do IVF, and I had eleven very promising embryos.

The doctor put in six. He told Dean and me, "You might have triplets. Just preparing you."

"Okay," I said.

I mean, what else was I supposed to say?

But I firmly believe things happen for a reason. Not one of those six embryos stuck. At the time, I was devastated. So, we tried again; they put in the other five.

And none of them stuck, either.

THE CLINIC (OR IS IT A SPA?)

When I was in my early twenties, I was only loved if I was thin, if I looked a certain way. If the scale showed more than 103 pounds, I wouldn't leave the house.

I'd take fifteen or twenty laxatives at a time. I took fen-phen. I ate a Slim Fast bar for breakfast, a Slim Fast bar for lunch, and like, five pieces of sushi for dinner. And that was it.

I needed to look good because of Nancy. She had not an ounce of body fat on her, so you'd think she'd relate—but when I said, "I think I look great," Nancy told me I was becoming too thin, and that I should get help.

When I found out I could spend thirty days at an eating dis-order clinic, my first thought was, *well, that would get me away from Dean.*

"Sure," I said. "I'm anorexic. I'm in."

I didn't really believe I was anorexic. I didn't care about get-ting better, because I thought I was fine. But I was looking at it as a retreat, like being at a spa. Like a mini-vacation from Dean; that's how bad my marriage was.

An eating disorder clinic, I'd soon learn, was not a spa. There were no massages, no fancy skin treatments. The clinic was in a wing of a hospital. There were about a dozen of us, and everyone ex-cept me had issues with overeating. Overeating and undereating fell under the same umbrella; we were treated using the same methods.

Our regime was harsh. We got up at 5:45 every morning and went for a walk. Then it was intense therapy, all day, every day. I knew the reasons behind my issues; I just didn't want to address them. So I just went along with the therapy, in the meantime feeling miserable.

We couldn't watch TV or make phone calls. Our meals, of course, were strictly rationed; there was no choice in what we were given to eat. There was another patient who had full-out bulimia. She hung out in my room to throw up after every meal.

They had "Family Night," when our families came to visit and participate in therapy. We were separated from our own families, placed in groups with other families. I later learned that in her group, Nancy was butchered! The other patients hated her for how she treated me. Afterward, she took to her bed for two days, popping Xanax, to recover from the verbal attack.

I was 103 pounds when I arrived and 118 when I left, thirty days later. When I got home, I freaked out about my weight. I went right back to not eating.

For much of our marriage, I didn't work. I had no need to, because Dean made plenty of money. He was on the road for work every Monday through Wednesday. On Wednesday nights, when he got home, he went out right away to play basketball. Thursdays, he worked all day, then played softball. Fridays, he worked in the morning, then played tennis. Weekends meant more sports. I didn't see much of him, which made our marriage bearable for me.

I remember when *Sex and the City* first came on. I loved that show; I couldn't get enough of it. But it made me think. My emotions about my husband were nothing like what Carrie, Samantha, Charlotte, and Miranda felt for the men in their lives.

I'd married somebody who didn't know how to give love or show love. And, looking back, maybe I was kinda the same. I wasn't mean and abusive like Dean was, but I didn't give of myself—to him or anyone else.

It's no surprise, really, that I felt so alone. I didn't even love myself. I was trying to look and be like Aunt Nancy. I was trying to shop and do the things she did. I didn't have kids, and I was too old to be a college girl. I just didn't fit in anywhere.

I don't think I knew who I was, at this point.

You can't fall in love, can't give love to somebody else, if you don't have a certain amount of love for yourself.

"Love is not something you look for.
Love is something you become."
- Alina Villasante

YES, AS A MATTER OF FACT...I *DO* HAVE TALENT!

I was 22 when I started taking every acting class I could find. I'd decided that I wanted to be in commercials.

Recently, I dug up a few studio shots of myself from that time. A makeup artist, Fernando, had done my makeup so I could get the shots done. In those pictures, I look pretty, but not all that happy. Looking at them now, I see sadness in my eyes. There was no sparkle.

Nonetheless, I went on some auditions, and I booked a few things. I didn't really know how to audition properly. I learned to, although it wasn't easy. But I had a great eye for talent, and I loved meeting people and talking with them, back then, same as I do now. I realized I could see myself working in talent…just not in front of the camera.

One Friday, I auditioned for a taco commercial. The next morning, I saw in the newspaper that T.R. Durphy Casting had just opened an office at Greenwich Studios (which, as a side note, is where Flipper used to be filmed).

I just auditioned for him yesterday, I thought. *Now I know T.R. Maybe I could go see his office.*

Some coincidences you just can't explain. Later that day, I was at a wedding, and who should show up but T.R. He recognized me from the taco commercial audition.

"Congratulations on opening your new business," I said.

"Yeah, it's cool," he replied.

"I don't think I got the taco commercial," I told him.

He smiled. "Yeah, maybe not. But you've got a lot of heart. You'll get something."

I kept thinking about it, and a few weeks later, I called him.

"Are you hiring?" I asked.

He said, "Actually, I am."

T.R. was a casting director. He hired me as his assistant. It changed my life, that job. Now I was auditioning people for national commercials. I was 27 years old, and for the first time ever, I felt like my life had purpose.

I forgot all about Dean. How he treated me mattered a lot less, now that I was spending my days around people I wanted to be with. I worked long hours, staying away from Dean as much as possible.

I was good at being a casting director. And honestly, that job was a huge ego trip for me. In Miami, if you were in the talent industry, people looked at you like you were God. I'd say to some wannabe actor, "I can't give you the job, but I have the ability to put you on tape. I have the ability to tell my clients about you." I was their foot in the door, and that power gave me a huge high.

I remember some years later, I was doing a SAG National commercial. By that point, I'd become an agent. The commercial was for kitty litter, and the request was for no blondes; they wanted brunettes only.

I said, "You know what? Redheads book everything." So I asked them, "Can I bring in Kelly Parks?"

"No," the client replied. "I said brunettes."

"You said not blonde," I reminded her. "And she's not blonde. Just bring her in."

And, of course, Kelly booked the friggin' SAG National. I was so damn proud of myself.

There was another guy, Michael Yo, who was a radio personality in Miami. He used to do *Access Hollywood*. A commercial was looking for funny sumo wrestlers, so I suggested him.

"He's not a damn sumo wrestler," they told me.

"He's half Korean," I said. "He's a personality on TV. And he's a little chubby." And he ended up booking it.

The whole thing swelled my head. I would walk into places and know they had to be nice to me because I was a casting director's assistant. If you're an agent, you need the casting director; that person is your lifeblood. So, when I called someone for their talent, and in some cases, it literally changed their lives—that completely fed my ego.

It fulfilled everything I wasn't getting at home.

In that business, there was a lot of spin. I remember being asked to judge the Miss Florida USA Pageant. I wasn't their first choice, but everybody else they wanted was out of town.

But nobody knew that. My bio said things like, "She's a swimmer." Okay, yeah, I liked going to the beach. "She's an oceanographer." Sure, I found marine life interesting.

That sort of thing wasn't at all unusual, in that business. There was a lot of embellishment.

But looking back now, it feels like the embellished version, not the real Marni, was what made me happy. I should have been happy being the real me, instead of this made-up version.

"WE DON'T DO DEPRESSION HERE."

Dean and I were still spending a lot of time with my Aunt Nancy and Uncle Jerry. When we went to Aunt Nancy's for dinner, she was always on schedule. If you were a minute late, she wouldn't look at you. You had to be there on time, eat with perfect manners, and, of course, look great.

You couldn't show any emotion, unless it was happiness. And fake happiness was perfectly acceptable. The day I found out one of my IVF rounds didn't work happened to be my cousin Ross's birthday. That night, we were at a restaurant, and of course, I was devastated. I could think of nothing except my failed IVF.

Aunt Nancy snapped her fingers in my face. "Uh, uh. We don't do depression here."

One time, I borrowed a pair of her leggings without asking first, and I stretched them out. She went crazy, yelling at me. The next time I went to the Jockey Club, the gate guard told me,

"You're not allowed in." Aunt Nancy and Uncle Jerry banned me from their condo complex because I borrowed her clothes.

She craved an audience. I had to sit there and watch Nancy when she did things like try on gowns. I had to be upbeat. I might be miserable and upset, but I had to look thin, smile, and tell her how gorgeous she looked.

I was supposed to go to my friend Carrie's wedding. Aunt Nancy was best friends with Carrie's mom. The two families were friends, although Carrie and I separately became friends outside the family thing. But her wedding was small, and she couldn't invite everyone, so she didn't invite Uncle Jerry's kids.

Because Jerry's children were not invited, Nancy said to me, "You cannot go to that wedding."

I did not go. In retrospect, I wish I'd said, "I'm fuckin' going anyway. I don't care what you say."

It was inappropriate for her to tell me what to do like that. But I was also a grownup. I allowed that to happen, and I own that now.

WHO *IS* THIS GUY?

In 1999, Dean lost his insurance license, because of the fraud. He told everyone, including me, that he was wrongly accused of false allegations.

But that didn't deter him. He said to this guy he knew, Jay, "Here's the deal. I'll pay you five hundred dollars a week to let me use your name. All you have to do is get your insurance license. Then I could go out as Jay Goldman."

Jay Goldman agreed to this, which kind of surprised me. Who was this guy?

Great question! More on that in the next chapter.

ASK YOURSELF...

- Have you ever felt pressured to date someone because they met someone else's expectations of who you "should" date? What did you do? If it happened today, would you handle it differently?
- Are there people in your life who take you for granted? What are you getting from those relationships? If they're unequal, is there a way to equalize the relationship, or would it be better to step away?
- What does it feel like when you let someone else control your state of mind? How can you take charge of your feelings and your emotional growth?

CHAPTER 5

THE EGO WANTS, BUT THE SOUL NEEDS

ONE OF THE GUYS

I met Jay in early 1999. He played on the same softball team as Dean. Every Sunday morning and Thursday night, all the wives and girlfriends would watch the guys play softball.

Jay was so cute, sort of Noah Wyle meets Sean Penn. I thought he had a gentle nature and a great sense of humor. He was completely different from loudmouth Dean.

I couldn't help flirting with Jay.

He was married to a woman named Ellen, and they had a daughter, Ashley, who was four when I met Jay. Ashley loved me; I was like a Spice Girl to her. I didn't have children at the time, and I loved hanging out with Ashley at softball games. She called me her "big sister."

By then, I was feeling a little better about myself. Working at a job I loved, as T.R. Durphy's assistant casting director, helped me tremendously. I was auditioning people for commercials and having lots of fun doing it. In many ways, it was the best time of my life.

Other than watching softball games—and God knows I didn't go to see my husband play—I was pretty much ignoring Dean. I was all but pretending I wasn't married to him.

One day, I worked up my nerve and called Jay to ask him out. "I don't think that's a good idea," he said.

"All right. Forget it." I hung up, embarrassed that I'd asked.

But a few days later, he called me back. "Actually, yeah. Let's meet for a drink."

AN AFFAIR TO REMEMBER

Jay and I started seeing each other, having an affair. I was very different from Ellen, and I knew that contrast appealed to him. She was restrictive with him, whereas I would tell him, "Do whatever you want."

In retrospect, that was just a role I played. I wasn't as interested in being Marni as I was in *not* being Ellen. I observed Ellen and thought, *if I want this guy, I have to be the complete opposite of her.*

Over time, I learned everything about Jay. When he was small, his biological father had abandoned the family, same as mine had. His mother remarried and his stepfather, Seymour, adopted Jay, but Seymour wasn't interested in being a father. There was another family Jay was close to, and the dad in that family, Jon, was a father figure for Jay. But for the most part, Jay told me, he raised himself. I totally understood what that was like.

Soon after college graduation, Jay married his girlfriend at the time. But it didn't work out, and they got a divorce. Not long afterward he married someone else, but that didn't work out, either; they were divorced within the year. Then he met and married Ellen, who was six years older than him.

He was involved in commercial real estate; he managed properties. But he was financially tied to Ellen, who was a divorce attorney. She had all the resources, and frankly, Jay seemed scared of her.

In an effort to be "not-Ellen," I put Jay on a pedestal. I made him think he was a king. I lived to make him happy.

Sometimes, Jay would go away for the weekend with Ellen and Ashley, on spontaneous last-minute trips. Or he'd be doing something else, like playing a softball game, and I could tell I was the last thing on his mind.

On the surface, I'd pretend that didn't bother me in the least. But deep inside, the emotional pain was intolerable.

How could he just forget about me? I'd wonder. *How could he not even answer my calls?*

But men and boys are not mind readers. You know that saying about how men are from Mars and women are from Venus? On Mars, they're well-versed in sports, sex, money, and food. That's it. On Venus, there are so many other aspects to our lives.

But what happens on Mars—I'm telling you, don't take it personally. A guy might be thinking about you, but he's also thinking about his sporting event the next day. And he'll call you after it's over.

How do you become okay with that? Back then, I wouldn't have been able to tell you, but now I'd say you fill your life with other things that matter to you, other passions. Your work or school. Your friends, your family. Fitness, hobbies, creative pursuits. You can appreciate men, sure; just don't expect the world from them.

I know that sounds really clichéd. I get it, we're all supposed to be equals now. We're supposed to treat everyone exactly the same. But I believe, at least in most cases, that men and women are wired differently from one another. The more I've come to terms with that, the less disappointed in men I've been.

"The flower doesn't dream of the bee. It blossoms and the bee comes."
— Mark Nepo

Back then, early in my affair with Jay, I'd catch myself looking at the phone a million times a day. *Why didn't he call me back?*

If I didn't hear from Jay, I felt like I couldn't move. If he didn't call me all day, the attitude and the nastiness I would exude were remarkable—remarkably awful, I mean. My happiness was contingent on hearing his voice.

I know this makes our relationship sound toxic. But honestly, it wasn't. I'll readily admit that not all aspects of it were healthy, but Jay and I always had a connection, a deep one. We were lovers, but we were also the best of friends.

Dean had no idea what was going on. Jay would come over to my place every Monday through Wednesday, while Dean was traveling for work. When Dean was home, he was in his own world, and it had nothing to do with me. Tennis, softball, ESPN. His whole world was sports.

Sunday nights were depressing for me, because they represented everybody, including Jay, with their families at home. I'd see Jay at softball on Sunday mornings, then he would leave with his wife and daughter.

But sometimes all the players and their significant others would go out. Those times, Jay and I would play footsie under the table. We were in the same community; we saw each other a lot with other people around. Part of the thrill of our affair was having this big secret no one knew about.

"THIS IS OUR BABY."

I know the exact date when our daughter, Taylor, was conceived, because it was the day the shooting happened at Columbine High School in Colorado: April 20, 1999.

I was with Jay, and we had been watching coverage of the story, shocked and silent. Finally, we turned it off and faced one another.

Jay kissed me.

"I'm ovulating," I told him.

"Okay," he replied.

So it was the pull-out method. Afterward, he said, "Maybe that wasn't such a good idea."

"Don't worry," I said. "I'll never get pregnant. I've done in vitro; I've done IUI. I can't conceive."

A week later, I could tell something was up with my body. A week after that, I thought, *I'm frickin' pregnant...I'm sure of it.*

I bought a pregnancy test, and the results couldn't have been more positive. I was stunned. Dean and I had tried everything to conceive, but with Jay, it happened effortlessly.

I don't know how Dean thought the baby was his. At that point, sex with him was sporadic, at best. We'd pretty much just let our sex life go. But everybody thought the baby was Dean's.

Jay's wife Ellen sent me a card that said, "Congratulations on finally getting pregnant!"

Oh, my God.

I gained eighty pounds when I was pregnant. Maybe that's why Ellen was friendly with me; she probably liked this happily chubby version of me.

Looking back now, it amazes me that Jay and I spent almost the entire first year of our relationship having an affair, and with me being pregnant. Weight gain, hormones, and hotel rooms! I don't know how we pulled it off. I remember *begging* Jay to get me a card, a present, to say, "I love you." Anything to prove his love for me.

He was a drug, and I was an addict.

The evening after I gave birth to Taylor—you couldn't make this story up. I'd had the baby during the day, and now it was about eight at night. Dean was leaving the hospital. He'd been there all day, of course, but he was over it by now.

When the elevator came to take Dean down to the first floor, Jay got off. It was like a director yelled, "Cue Jay. Exit Dean. And…action!"

Jay came into my room and exclaimed over the baby. "Can I hold her?"

I handed her over. It was just the three of us in the room.

"This is your baby," I said. "This is our baby."

So now I had Taylor, who was then (and still is) the spitting image of Jay. But I was married to Dean, and he thought Taylor was his.

I remember saying to myself, "What else am I gonna do? Where else can I go?"

Nobody had emphasized to me the importance of educa-tion, of college. No one ever told me to build a career so I could take care of myself, and any dependents who came along. The message was always just, "Marry someone for money." So that's what I'd done. I knew my salary as a casting director's assistant wouldn't even begin to cover my expenses, if I told Dean the truth and Taylor and I were on our own.

After Taylor was born, I looked at my pre-pregnancy clothes, and they looked like things that would fit an American Girl doll, not things that would ever fit me. I wanted to have liposuction, but wisely, my friend Lisa suggested I hire a trainer instead. I worked out with the trainer four times a week. We would walk the 3.1 miles around Aventura Circle (a walking path surrounding a golf course), then work out in a gym. I resolved to do whatever it took to become "Sexy Marni" again.

When Taylor was nine months old, Jay's mother, Dianne, came to visit. At a softball game, she asked, "Can I hold the baby?"

Taylor took to Dianne right away. It was as if she could tell this was her grandmother.

Attending those softball games became even more agonizing. It had been hard enough before I was a mom, but now—watching Jay go home with Ellen and Ashley, and I was with Dean, who wasn't Taylor's father—it broke my heart.

When Dean would hold Taylor, I could never bring myself to smile. I just couldn't.

Around that time, Jay went on a family cruise with his parents, Ellen, and Ashley. Every time he would leave for a trip like that, he'd turn his phone off. And I admit I went bat-shit. At the time, I didn't know it was abandonment issues that were triggering me. I learned that years later, in therapy.

While on the cruise, Jay confessed to his mother that Taylor was his. He told me about it later. They were alone on an excursion, sitting on a picnic bench on some island, and he broke the news. But he also told her he no longer had anything to do with me. He claimed that I was content staying with Dean. He said Dean was a good provider, and Taylor would want for nothing. He told Dianne that our affair had been brief, and it was now over.

That was bullshit, of course. Dean was still traveling part of every week, and Jay continued to come over when Dean was gone. Whenever Jay was at my place, he treated Taylor like she was his little girl, but as she grew, of course she didn't know the authenticity of it. I'm sure he just seemed like a nice man who hung out with her mommy sometimes.

As for Dianne, I guess she didn't tell Ellen because she wanted Jay and Ellen to be together. She knew that if Ellen knew about Taylor, all hell would break loose.

MOVIN' OUT

I'd like to say there was some insightful moment or dramatic fight that finally made me leave Dean, but there really wasn't. It was more like, one day I simply decided to get on with my life.

So I moved out. Lorie helped me move. It was the spring of 2001, and Taylor had just turned a year old. I rented a small condo at the Bay Club, a high-rise building in Aventura. Jay, Ellen, and Ashley lived in another part of Aventura, in a townhouse.

Jay told me he would leave Ellen, but he needed thirty more days. But then thirty days passed, and he said he needed another thirty. Then thirty more, and thirty more. I became increasingly hysterical. Back then, I didn't know what a "trigger" was. I had no idea that Jay's behavior was a reminder to me of the many instances of abandonment in my youth.

Although Jay kept making excuses not to leave Ellen, he was completely supportive of me leaving Dean. He told me, "Marni, if you're gonna get divorced, call Danny Kaplan. He's a great divorce attorney."

So I did. But after we met and talked about my case, Danny said, "Do you mind if I don't represent you? I can help you find someone else, but I'd rather not represent you…because I really would like to date you."

I laughed. "Okay. Cool."

We started dating. I liked Danny, though I didn't take the relationship seriously. My heart still belonged to Jay.

One morning, Jay saw my car at Danny's place. And that was it for him; he left Ellen that night. He couldn't stand the idea of me being with someone else. He came to my condo in the Bay Club, and I was ecstatic. I thought we were going to be together, were going to get married.

That lasted exactly three months: June through September of 2001. Then he went back to Ellen, telling her that he and I were just friends, that there was nothing between us.

Why? Well, remember what I said earlier, that it always seemed like he was kind of scared of Ellen?

Yeah. That.

My mother had come back into my life when I was pregnant. She was in the delivery room when Taylor was born.

After Taylor's birth, every Tuesday, Aunt Nancy, my mother, and I would take Taylor to the Aventura Mall. We would have lunch and shop; Tuesday was "girls' day." Nancy adored Taylor; she couldn't get enough of her. She would feed Taylor a bottle with one hand and hold a martini in the other.

Nancy was generous when she wanted to be. When we went shopping, I always came home with makeup or clothes.

Unfortunately, I didn't enjoy those days. I spent most of my time pushing Taylor's stroller through the mall and crying on the phone to Jay about why we weren't together. I wasted such precious time, time that I'll never get back, because I wasn't living in the moment.

Back then, we had pagers. We didn't have texting on our phones; we used pagers to stay in touch. The nights Jay didn't spend with me, I found myself unable to get out of bed the next day—unable to start my day—unless I saw a beep on my pager from Jay. I'd be rocking my daughter and staring at the little pager.

If there was nothing from Jay, I would just sit there and cry.

Jay was so inconsistent with his beeps. I still saw him on softball days, but after he left softball with Ellen and Ashley, I might not hear from him for hours. All I did was cry and wait for a page, playing with Taylor. I will never forget that pain.

I was still working part time for T.R. It was one of the hardest points of my life; I had no stability and a little girl to raise. T.R.'s best friend, Paul, who was a head-shot photographer, shared office space with us. T.R., his boyfriend Don, Paul,

"I love people who make me laugh. I honestly think it's the thing I like most, to laugh. It cures a multitude of ills. It's probably the most important thing in a person."
- Audrey Hepburn

and Paul's boyfriend Anthony became my family. The hysterical laughter all day with them made my horrific situation okay.

As I look back on that now, it reminds me that finding your people is crucial! I'd never have made it if I wasn't doing what I loved, surrounded by people I loved.

On the days I worked, my mother watched Taylor. Her life revolved around her granddaughter. Her house was set up with toys and dolls; it looked like a preschool.

But at night, Michelle herself was working. And what did she do? Well, it shouldn't surprise you. She was almost 60 by then, but still gorgeous. She worked for an escort service.

I remember that she actually said to me, "Marni, just be a call girl. You go on dates anyway, right? If you fool around with a guy, you fool around with him. Might as well make money for it."

Unbelievable!

But it's not all that different, really, from what Aunt Nancy said. The only difference was that Aunt Nancy's message was more legitimate: "Marry the rich guy."

And my mom was saying, "You don't need to marry the rich guy. You need the rich guy, you just don't need to marry him."

But either way, you're not being true to yourself. There's absolutely no self-respect involved with either of those approaches.

My mother and aunt are both crazy. Just slightly different types of crazy.

"HOW BAD CAN IT BE?"

Nonetheless, I was struggling financially. I loved my job, but I didn't make enough to pay my bills. Dean provided child support, but it didn't stretch as far as I needed it to.

So I called Laurence, that disgusting-but-rich guy I'd dated before I met Dean. He was thrilled to hear from me, and he wanted to see me right away.

I told Laurence, "I'll go out with you, but only if we can fly first class to New York and stay at the Waldorf Astoria." I didn't think he'd take me seriously. I couldn't believe he called my bluff, but he did.

I left Taylor with Dean and flew off to New York, first class with somebody vile. I can only imagine what the flight attendants thought of me.

Laurence had reserved a spacious, apartment-like suite at the Waldorf Astoria. It was the hugest hotel suite I'd ever seen in Manhattan. I think Paris Hilton was staying next door.

We took a walk on Fifth Avenue and window-shopped. Of course, he didn't buy me a thing. And I certainly didn't have the funds to shop there!

Back at the hotel, I told Laurence that I didn't feel good. I went in another room to get away from him.

I can't be here, I thought. *I have to leave, I have to leave, I have to leave.*

I went back out, and he glared at me. I knew what he wanted, what he expected, and if he didn't get it, I truly thought he might kill me. The creepiest chill went through my entire body.

"Excuse me," I whispered. I slipped into the bathroom, with my cellphone in my pocket.

I called the airline and said, "I need a ticket to Miami immediately. Can you please get me off the Sunday flight and onto one tomorrow morning? I have to get out of here right away."

Once my flight was arranged, I called hotel security to escort me out. Laurence was furious when security showed up at the door, but what could he do? Downstairs, I hopped into the first cab I saw, and told the driver to head toward the Holland Tunnel.

I call my mother from the cab. "I'm leaving," I told her. "It's horrible."

And she said, "How bad could it be?"

Oh, my God. I hung up on her.

Looking back, it shouldn't have surprised me to hear my mother say that. She'd go out with anyone who had money, after all.

And Aunt Nancy, God love her, had married horrible Uncle Jerry because he was a successful guy. If I'd been talking to Aunt Nancy in the cab, she too would have said, "How bad could it be?"

My brother Andy was living in New Jersey at this time. I called him from the cab, but he was incoherent. He was mumbling; I had no idea what he was saying.

I called my lifeline: Jay. He stayed on the phone with me the entire time, trying to get me to calm down. I'd never been so scared in my life; I couldn't shake the terror I'd felt when I was alone with Laurence.

I later learned that my brother and my mother, who never spoke on the phone, were at this point talking to each other, both of them slamming me for leaving the hotel.

"How could she leave him?" they asked each other. "What's so bad about being in a penthouse suite at the Waldorf?"

By then, I'd arrived at my brother's house. Andy was doing a lot of drugs at that time, and he was completely irrational. He began ranting at me, and he handed his phone to our mother so she could rant at me, too.

What is going on here? I thought. *Who are these two people attacking me?*

Then I realized I'd left my wallet in the cab.

My brother's wife was out of the country on business, but her family was there, helping Andy take care of their four-year-old daughter. Her father and sister drove me to LaGuardia. They gave me some cash, and somehow, I got on a plane. I don't know how or why they let me on without identification, but they did.

How I survived that night, I will never know. I can still hear my mother saying, "How bad could it be? How bad could it be?"

It was such a vile experience. That feeling, knowing I almost allowed myself to be used like a piece of meat—it was awful.

Looking back, even though I had to take all that shit from my family, I'm glad I listened to my instincts. I will never doubt I did the right thing, getting out of there.

IS IT WORTH IT?

Want to hear something funny about Laurence? He's this huge Miami sports fan, and he shows up at lots of major sporting events. He's always decked out in team garb, and the cameras pan in on him all the time.

When I see him on TV and I'm with Taylor and her friends, I tell them, "See him? That's what I had to do at nineteen. I had to go out with that guy, because I had no means of supporting myself. That's what happens when you don't get an education, when you rely on other people to take care of you. Don't do that, girls."

At 19, I went out with Laurence for survival. Going out with him at that age was gross, but going out with him again at age 32 was over the top. No matter how bad things were, there was no reason for me to do that. There's no reason any girl or woman should do a thing like that.

I wanted to have the high life. I wanted to fly first class and stay in a penthouse suite. I wanted to pretend I wasn't a struggling single mom, in love with a guy who wouldn't leave his wife to be with me and the child we'd created.

Sure, I wanted the high life. But what was I mortgaging? I was mortgaging my true self.

You have to decide—is it worth it? Is discarding your self-esteem worth it, just to gain prestige and material possessions?

That was a huge learning experience for me. I refused to sell my soul to be with somebody like that. If I did, I would have paid for it, emotionally, every day thereafter.

I wouldn't have put it in these terms back then, but what I was doing during that horrible, horrible night was staying true to myself.

EVERYTHING IS TEACHING ME A LESSON.

Remembering this incident feels ridiculously embarrassing. Here I was, 32 years old and still learning.

And now I'm 49, and I'm still learning. I guess we're all still learning.

WHAT FRIGGIN' NEXT?

Taylor and I continued to live in that condo at the Bay Club. I was still casting, but only on an as-needed basis. It was impossible to make ends meet on such a small income. Money was a huge worry for me in those days.

Around this time, Jay began proceedings to divorce Ellen. But that wasn't because of Taylor and me. He still didn't want Ellen to know about our affair, to know Taylor was his. I'm sure he worried that if Ellen found out, she wouldn't let him see Ashley.

His plans to divorce had nothing to do with me. It was simply that he was miserable being married to Ellen.

Since things were going nowhere with Jay, I started dating a guy named Steven. We were together for half of 2002 and the first few months of 2003. Then I got pregnant. I wasn't sure what to do. Steven didn't want to marry me, which, of course, brought up more feelings of abandonment in me.

The problem solved itself when I started hemorrhaging. It was so scary. I was at Steven's place. I left, taking myself to the emergency room. They treated me, and physically I was fine, but in the meantime, I had a full-on panic attack. What would happen to Taylor, if something unspeakable happened to me?

But I recovered and I called Jay, who came to the hospital to take me home. On my door was an eviction notice—because Steven, who had paid my rent the month prior, hadn't paid for the current month. He neglected to tell me he'd stopped paying my rent.

I was furious. What next? What friggin' next?

SAME SHIT, DIFFERENT DAY

With nowhere else to go, I packed up and went to a friend's place for a few weeks. Then Jay came to the rescue. He got Taylor and me a one-bedroom apartment in Hollywood Beach.

In a weird coincidence, both of our divorces, mine from Dean and his from Ellen, became final around that same time. I said to him, "Why are we not married? Our divorces are final. We don't have to tell Ellen that Taylor is yours. We can pretend we started seeing each other after your divorce."

So, we got married at a courthouse. He was reluctant, but he agreed because I wanted it so badly.

Happy ending, right? Not so fast.

During this time, my mother was still watching Taylor regularly. She'd be so anxious, calling me at work a dozen times a day to ask when I was coming home.

"What does it matter?" I'd respond. "Where else do you have to be?"

She *didn't* have to be anywhere—and since I was on the clock, only getting paid for the few hours I worked, it was aggravating to have her pressuring me to come home. But beggars couldn't be choosers; I had no one else to watch Taylor.

One day in June, I went over to her apartment. She wasn't watching Taylor that day; in fact, she wasn't even home. I let myself in, figuring I'd wait for her.

The phone rang, and I answered it.

"Michelle?" some guy asked.

Curious, I pretended to be her. "Yeah?"

"Can I come over?"

Carefully, I said, "Yeah, sure."

He replied, "But not in front of the kid. We're not doing candy in front of the kid."

Whoa. By "doing candy," he definitely did not mean sitting around eating chocolate bars.

And "the kid" was my daughter.

I went into a psychotic rage, breaking things in my mother's apartment, screaming and hyperventilating. I then went on a pilgrimage, looking for her. I found her in an upscale neighborhood—doing crack, of course.

Immediately, I took Taylor to the pediatrician. She was fine, thank God. But I couldn't believe it. I really thought my mother had gotten it out of her system and she wouldn't go back. This is a woman who hardly ever drank. She never smoked pot, never did anything else. Instead, she went straight to the worst thing she could possibly do.

As a teen, I'd lived through my mother on crack. But to do that to a three-year-old you supposedly adored? It was unfathomable.

I went back to my mother's place. And it wasn't long before there was banging on the door. I looked through the peephole and heard a familiar voice yelling, "Marni! I see you in there! Get out!"

It was fucking Jerry Blair, *throwing me out again*, this time from my mother's apartment. I called Nancy, who was no help. She hadn't wanted to deal with this type of thing in 1987, much less in 2003.

After that, my mother disappeared. I was so pissed at her, I didn't even care. I resolved to focus on my marriage to Jay, our daughter, and my work, and forget about everything else.

But Ellen was still in the picture; she was, after all, the mother of Jay's other child. She would say to him, "Why did you marry Marni, of all people? Ashley is miserable. She hates the idea of you being married to someone else."

So, three months after we got married—around the same

time I found out my mother was on crack again—Jay served me with divorce papers. He told me, "I need us to get divorced, but it will be a 'paper divorce.' We'll still be together."

He didn't give me any choice in the matter. He divorced me to prove to his eight-year-old daughter and his ex-wife that we weren't married.

That was a tough time. I went on autopilot. I internalized all my feelings, and did my best to go about my life.

Jay would tell Ellen, Ashley, and his parents that, "There's no Marni." But he was with me most of the time. He was more or less still living with me.

We were together, then not together, then together again. It was very dysfunctional.

I think now about the contrast between what happened with Laurence and what I felt for Jay. Laurence had been all about my ego. It was about wanting someone to give me status and luxury.

But my feelings for Jay reached much deeper into my soul. He wasn't just what I wanted. He was what my soul needed.

AGENTING—AND ADULTING

I hated my tiny apartment. Taylor and I spent that Christmas at Lorie's big, beautiful house in Cooper City, about a half-hour from Aventura. I felt right at home. I wished I could live there with Taylor.

Lorie introduced me to a guy named Jason. My eyes lit up when I heard his parents lived in a penthouse in Williams Island, a prestigious resort community. Jason had beautiful green eyes and a fun personality. I knew he was in AA, and I believed he no longer drank.

We started dating, and soon afterward, Taylor and I moved into Jason's place. He lived in yet another building on Aventura Circle. By then I'd probably lived on just about every section of that circle.

Jason was cute, but I didn't know the severity of his psychotic problems and his alcoholism. I took such a risk living with a stranger.

Then T.R. decided to close his office. I was out of a job.

I went home and called my friend Lisa. She was an agent at the Green Agency, a talent agency on South Beach. She got me a job there.

Agenting was a natural fit for me. As a casting director, I'd called agents to request various talent they represented. So I already knew a lot of the talent from auditioning them. I knew who would be good at what. What the clients would think of this person or that one. How each actor auditioned. I already had that knowledge in my back pocket, and it paid off.

The job was full time, with great benefits. I drove an hour to and from work, but it was worth it. I loved the job; I had the best time working there.

Things on the home front weren't as good. I finally realized what a mess Jason was. It got really bad one night. Jason was drunk, yelling at me, and I was scared for myself and for Taylor.

I called Jay and asked him to call 911. He didn't want his voice to be on a recorded 911 call about me (yeah, still scared of Ellen), so he called my old boss, T.R., and had him dial 911. The police came and got Taylor and me out of there.

Jay found me another apartment, again on Hollywood Beach. I tried to settle in. Jay lived in a different building on Hollywood

Beach, about a half-mile from mine. Whenever he came over, he made the trip via rollerblades. That way, Ellen wouldn't happen to drive by my place and see his car parked there.

He was such a friggin' scaredy-cat.

Not long after this, Dean went to jail. There had been an undercover operation for months within the FDLE (Florida Department of Law Enforcement). When Dean was arrested, I was horrified! Stealing from the elderly? Oh, my God! I was deposed, and FDLE rightfully concluded that I was completely clueless. Dean, his brother, and his cousin all went into the slammer for a few years.

Taylor was barely seeing him anymore, though he still thought she was his daughter, so it didn't affect her much. But I did take calls from him (when he was permitted to make them), and it made him happy to hear Taylor's little voice over the line.

A HOUSE IN THE 'BURBS

Soon after Taylor's fourth birthday, I said to Jay, "Please, finally, can we get married and get a house?" And he agreed that yes, it was time for us to be together as a family.

We started house hunting, and in late spring we found a house in Cooper City—where Lorie lived, where I'd dreamed of moving and raising my family.

We were scheduled to close in July. We booked a date to get married on the beach, at The Breakers in Palm Beach. This was around the time I was a judge in the Miss Florida USA pageant, and I went around telling everybody at the pageant, "I'm getting married in Palm Beach next week." I was so happy.

The night before our wedding date, Jay took me to Macy's to

get a cute little beachy dress to wear the next day. For exercise, I was still walking the 3.1 miles around Aventura Circle, and after the dress shopping, we parted so I could go for my walk.

My phone rang soon after Jay drove away, and it was the man himself.

"I can't marry you," he said.

"What? *What?*"

"I can't marry you," Jay repeated. "My mother won't give me money for the house, for the mortgage, if I marry you."

I was speechless. I collapsed right there on the Circle, crying and screaming.

I went home and called Lorie to tell her what happened.

"I'm done," I told her. "I am so done with him."

"No, you're not," Lorie said. "You make sure you're there on closing day. You get in there and get your name on the deed. *Beg* him to marry you, if you have to—*but get your name on the fuck-ing deed to the house.*"

I didn't even know what a deed was. Patiently, she explained it to me. Then she said, "You're not on the mortgage, but you're gon-na own that house. To do that, your name has to be on the deed."

So I called Jay and told him to come over. And I said to him, "You're gonna marry me, because I want my name on that house. I'm not gonna live there with you without being married, and risk getting kicked out of my own house. We'll figure out the money thing, but we are in this together."

I guess I finally wore him down. The wedding on the beach was off, but in August of 2004, we closed on the house, with my name on the deed. And a friend who was a notary married us in our new, empty living room.

Finally, I had my house in the suburbs. Just what I'd always wanted. And I had Jay. We were married; we were a family.

My soul felt at ease. I was sure that every aspect of my life would be perfect from that day forward.

But if I've learned anything over the years, it's that God laughs when we make plans.

ASK YOURSELF...

- Have you ever been head-over-heels in love? Has it made you do things you knew you shouldn't? If so, how did that make you feel?
- What do we owe the people we love, and who love us back? What do they owe us in return?
- In what ways can you protect and take care of yourself, regardless of who else is in or out of your life?

CHAPTER 6

LOVE AND GUILT ARE NOT THE SAME

JUST ANOTHER SUBURBAN FAMILY

You know what really drove me to push Jay so hard about the house? It was when my friend Lisa said to me, "You gotta give Taylor the most boring life possible."

She was right. I wanted my daughter to have the stability I never had.

We moved to Cooper City, where Lorie lived. Cooper City, a suburb of Miami, is about a half-hour away from Aventura, the community I'd lived in for over a decade. Aventura was where I'd lived with Dean, where I met Jay, where we'd carried on our affair for years and years. It was actually quite a scandal when we left Aventura; things kind of blew up, and everyone was talking about us. Ellen was in complete shock, and the community rallied around her to offer support.

I didn't care. I was so excited. "I'm in the suburbs; I have neighbors. I have a pool."

But word gets around, and soon everyone in our new neighborhood knew about us, too. *Those new folks—they used to be married to other people, and they had an affair. Crazy, right?*

Walking in, Jay and I were like *Days of Our Lives*. A few people pretended to befriend me, but it was always, "So, tell me about it! What was it like, having an affair?"

I was happy to tell them everything. Anything, I thought, to be accepted here.

But during those years, I never met anyone with whom I truly connected. I'm me, and my interests might differ from those of other people. For instance, someone might say to me, "You going to the PTA meeting?" And I'd reply, "No. I have to go get my lashes done."

That being said, I never regretted living there, because it was great for Taylor. I didn't mind that I didn't fit in; my daughter did.

It's all about balance. I was making sacrifices for Taylor. When you have kids, you have to do that. It might not have been where I was happiest, but it worked out for Taylor.

Once we'd settled in, I started throwing around the suggestion of having another baby. I thought Taylor needed a sibling. Jay wasn't as into the idea, so we weren't actively trying, but in November, I got pregnant anyway.

As I had the first time, I gained a huge amount of weight during my second pregnancy. By the time I gave birth to Noah in August of 2005, I was over 200 pounds. But I saved my baby's life. (More on that later.)

After we got home from the hospital, I was appalled at my postpartum size. I was so ashamed of how I looked, I'd barely leave the house. I didn't even want to step out to get the mail.

On the rare occasions when I did go out, I'd only do so if I first put on sunglasses and lipstick. I'd wear big white t-shirts to hide my body. I was afraid people wouldn't like me if I didn't look perfect.

I did finally lose the baby weight. I didn't have a fancy trainer this time; I just starved myself and started going to Jazzercise every morning when Noah was four months old. But issues around body image continued to plague me. If my weight went over 125 pounds, I'd yell at my kids. I'd think, *oh my God, now I'm fat and nobody will love me.*

I took out my inner rage on my family. If I felt bloated after eating, I'd just snap. But I'd kind of resigned myself to it; I thought that's just who I was. I didn't know these were triggers of the emotional stuff I'd dealt with all my life.

I started to take the social layers in my neighborhood really personally. If I learned that someone was having a party and we weren't invited, I'd get upset and wonder: what makes them better than us?

The idea of throwing my own party was out of the question. Who would I invite?

My son didn't even have a bris. They cut him at the hospital.

WHO AM I NOW?

Throughout my pregnancy, I'd continued to work at the Green Agency. I worked until the day Noah was born. I'd planned to go back after six weeks, but I found I couldn't. Noah needed me. Taylor was five; she needed me, too.

But quitting my job was tough, because I lost that identity. I still tried to keep my hand in it. When I'd see some cute, charismatic kid, I'd say to the kid's parents, "Oh, gosh. You've got to call so-and-so-agent. Tell them Marni sent you."

I tried to live vicariously in that talent world. In later years, when it was career day at Taylor's school, I'd bring in scripts for the kids to read, just to give them a feel for it. I clung to that identity for a long time, because I believed it gave me status, gave me clout. But the reality was, I was a stay-at-home mom with a baby.

And my baby was not doing what a baby's supposed do.

Noah wouldn't nap. He wouldn't eat, wouldn't take a bottle. He started to throw up regularly.

At birth, he'd had an extra digit on one hand and a skin tag on the other. And on both feet, his second and third toes were webbed together. We'd had the extra digit and skin tag removed when he was four months old, but the doctors advised us to leave his feet the way they were.

There was something about my son that wasn't quite right. But I didn't know what it was.

FAMILY DRAMA

Noah was a challenging baby, and I needed help, so Jay's mother Dianne started coming over. She wasn't warm and fuzzy, but I was happy to have an extra set of hands around. But then Ellen gave Dianne an ultimatum: "You either see Noah or Ashley. Not both."

So Dianne told her, "Of course, I'm going to see Ashley." She kept coming over to my house, though. And one day, Ellen saw Noah's car seat in Dianne's car. She called Dianne a liar. She wanted Dianne to give up Noah completely.

As a result, Dianne and her husband, Seymour, discarded us. Like we were garbage.

I guess this shouldn't have surprised me. Dianne had never liked me. I remember the first Thanksgiving after Jay and I moved into our house. I wanted so badly to impress his parents. I wanted to make them a nice meal, show them how happy Jay and I were in our lovely home. I remember going all out, trying to cook a sumptuous meal and set a beautiful table. And Dianne just looked at me with disgust.

All she knew of me was that I came into Jay's world and got pregnant—and now Jay was with me, and Ellen was miserable.

At Dianne's house, there were pictures of Jay and Ellen all over the place, and tons of pictures of Ashley. There were none of me and none of baby Noah.

And definitely none of Taylor, because in all this time, Dianne never told Ellen that Taylor was Jay's. And Jay didn't tell Ellen, either.

Days of Our Lives, right?

Taylor was five, and she was just this perfect, perfect little everything. I worshiped her. She was like a delicious doll. When I contrasted how easy Taylor was with Noah's fussiness, it broke my heart. I couldn't stop worrying for him.

I was losing my shit. Jay called someone who called someone, and they found out my mother was clean again. She'd shown up at my baby shower for Noah, uninvited and totally out of it, and afterward, I'd assumed that was that; she was out of my life forever. But now she said she was clean and wanted to help take care of the baby. I insisted that she be drug tested. We even got her hair tested—everything. When it turned out she truly was clean, she became the only person I would let watch Noah. Even so, after that I stipulated that she still be tested sporadically, which she agreed to do.

All during the next year, when Taylor was in first grade, Jay worked with an attorney to try to legally adopt her. He wanted to legally adopt his own daughter.

Dean got out of jail that year, and I told him right away that he wasn't Taylor's dad. (When Jay and I got married the second time, I'd stopped accepting child support from Dean; I didn't need it by then, and Dean certainly didn't have it anyway.)

It was one of the most difficult things I ever had to do, making that phone call. But it had to be done.

Dean wasn't surprised, but he still asked me to get a DNA test. "Just look at her," I said.

He couldn't deny the resemblance, but he still wanted proof. So we got the DNA test.

All this time, Jay was telling his parents and Ellen, "There's no Marni." And he was telling me that his parents didn't want to see me, but also that, "There's no Ellen."

Uh-huh.

Then Dean told Ellen what I'd confessed, that Taylor was Jay's. He told her we'd done a DNA test to prove it. For the record, Ellen couldn't stand Dean, had never liked him—but she did believe every word he said about this. It was impossible to deny it, after all. I'm sure all the puzzle pieces fell into place for Ellen at that point.

But there wasn't anything Ellen could do about it, except continually increase Jay's child support for Ashley. She did that over and over. Not because she needed the money; it was just for revenge. Even though he never saw Ashley, Jay supported her financially until she was grown.

Jay's stepfather Seymour was a bit of an oddball. After I gave birth to Noah, as he was leaving the hospital Seymour said to me, "Goodbye, Noah's mother." That was it.

The only other time we had a conversation was one day over lunch. He asked me, "Why are you in love with Jay?"

I didn't even know how to answer that! If you're in love, you're in love—right?

Dianne and Seymour wouldn't let us come along when they saw Ashley. And Ashley visiting our home was out of the question. She was a preteen by then, so she had some say in the matter. She told her mother, "I don't want anything to do with them."

To this day, that's true. Jay has reached out over and over, but Ashley refuses to communicate with him.

Meanwhile, my in-laws embraced Noah secretly, like an affair. They were always good with him, but they didn't want to see Taylor. I never really understood their feelings (or lack thereof) about Taylor. Maybe they thought if I hadn't had Taylor, Jay's and my affair would have ended and he'd still be with Ellen. I guess they blamed that on Taylor, though it certainly wasn't her fault she was born under those circumstances.

Of course, when she was little Taylor didn't realize how much Dianne didn't like her. She wasn't aware of that until she was older. I recalled how affectionate Dianne had been with Taylor when she was a baby, when we'd see Dianne at softball games. It made me sad, thinking about how Taylor had responded to that. But back then, Dianne thought Dean was Taylor's dad. At that time, Dianne thought of Taylor simply as a cute baby who belonged to other people.

CHILD WITH A PROBLEM

In his last year of preschool, Noah still couldn't hold a crayon. He would isolate himself, wouldn't play with the other kids.

They had clocks and schedules at preschool, but the only way he could understand timeframes was if we said something like, "Watch one SpongeBob, then it will be time for [whatever was coming next]."

I took him to the pediatrician, and they said, "Let's wait it out. He'll grow out of it."

But Noah wasn't thriving. When the school year was up, I said to Jay, "He needs to do pre-K again, and go to kindergarten a year from now."

Jay wanted Noah to go to kindergarten because he didn't want to pay a thousand dollars a month anymore for preschool. So, we sent him, but when the school year was up, I insisted that he repeat kindergarten, and the school agreed. In fact, they thanked me, saying a lot of parents pushed their kids to advance when they weren't ready.

His second year of kindergarten, he was the oldest kid in the class. He was small and today, he's still small for his age. Because of his size, he didn't look all that different from the other kids in his class. But he sure acted different.

Still, nobody could tell me exactly what was going on with him. I had IEP meetings, parent-teacher meetings, and, of course, carpool. I was doing a lot of running around. Taylor was in Hip Hop Kids—a performance dance troupe—so I had to get her to dance lessons a few times a week after school. Noah would be melting by that time of day, but he had to go along wherever we were going. Today, I think I could do that running around calmly, but back then, I was all over the place.

I did all that on my own. Jay never went to school meetings. He did drive Taylor to sleepovers, parties, the mall, and things like that. If I could get out of those sorts of duties, I did. I'd later learn that I had undiagnosed social anxiety, so it makes sense that I didn't engage with the outside world when I didn't have to.

Year by year, Noah went through elementary school, but it was clear he couldn't handle the work or the social aspects. They looked at him like he was a problem child, not a child with a problem. Because he didn't have a diagnosis, his IEP (Individual Education Plan) was limited. There was only so much the school and teachers could do.

And, of course, some teachers were better with him than others.

He had a bracelet he wore all the time, this little beaded thing. He wore it as security; he always had it on. One time when he was about eight, we were in Vail and he dropped it in the snow. We thought it was lost forever, but the snow melted and we found it lying on the sidewalk—in the shape of a heart.

Then, when he was in fifth grade, I guess he was playing around with the bracelet too much in class, and the teacher thought he was being a distraction. She took it away. To Noah, it was like taking off his arm.

She gave it back, but after that, anytime he played with it, she'd take it from him again. It was really upsetting for him. So, we pulled him out of public school and put him in a special needs school.

I spoiled Noah, I admit it. Whatever he wanted, he got. He was little Prince Noah. If he wanted me to bake him a cake at two in the morning, I'd get my ass up and bake him a cake. I did that because I felt so much guilt.

But love and guilt are not the same thing.

Because he was small and quirky, he got bullied a lot in our neighborhood. I remember one time some kid was picking on him, and later, when I was driving with Noah in the car, I spotted the bully. I rolled down my car window and called out to him, "Don't you ever say another word to my son. *Ever.*"

An hour later, the police were at my door. Apparently, the bully's mother had reported me. I have no idea why. I didn't get out of my car. I didn't hit the kid, and I didn't even yell at him. Yet, the bully's mom had the police show up at my door.

I can't imagine doing that. If another parent had ever said something to Taylor like I said to that kid and Taylor came home and told me about it, she and I would have had a long talk about it. I'd get to the bottom of what happened. No way would I just call the cops on another parent!

A MEDICAL SLEUTH

In 2015, when Noah was ten, I took him to an endocrinologist. I thought they might have a solution for us. But the doctor said Noah was not growth deficient.

"He's the size of a postage stamp," I replied. "How can you say he's not growth deficient?"

The doctor just shook his head. "He's not."

The next year, I begged the doctor for a prescription to start Noah on growth hormones. He was becoming more and more aware of how kids teased him, and I thought if he were bigger, kids would stop picking on him.

One company sent us a trial kit and a home nurse. I was so excited, thinking that finally, Noah was going to grow. But his test results showed he wasn't growth deficient, and our insurance wouldn't cover growth hormones. We still had a prescription, and like lots of parents, we paid out of pocket. Once the prescription ran out, Jay had a client in Brazil who got Noah's growth hormones for us there and sent them to us. I argued with Jay a lot over that. I didn't feel comfortable acquiring something like that from outside the U.S.

I was so damn frustrated. I called the insurance company again, and they told me they couldn't cover growth hormones unless there was a genetic disorder.

Genetic? Hmm.

I "Web MD'd" everything I could find on genetics. In May of 2017, I called a pediatric geneticist and expressed my concerns. I thought maybe it was Fragile X, or something like that. The pediatric geneticist did basic bloodwork, and everything came back negative. But they wanted to do deeper analysis, including bloodwork for Jay and me—which made sense, if we were looking into potential genetic issues.

It took several months to process the results. Noah received a diagnosis—finally!—in September 2017. He has Smith Lemli Opitz Syndrome.

Smith Lemli Opitz Syndrome, or SLOS as it's known, arises when a particular gene combination makes it difficult for a fetus to metabolize the cholesterol it receives from its mother during pregnancy. We all hear about how bad cholesterol supposedly is for us, but that's not entirely true. Humans need a certain amount of cholesterol to survive. When a fetus is developing in the womb, it needs quite a bit. A fetus afflicted with SLOS doesn't get enough cholesterol, which causes problems at birth and further down the line.

Every kid born with SLOS has an extra digit and webbed toes. But no one said anything about that when Noah was born; they just thought it was some small quirk of nature. We'd had his extra digit and a skin tag surgically removed, as I mentioned earlier.

When the genetic counselor said both of us needed to be tested, Jay was certain it came only from me. But she told him it would take both parents being carriers for SLOS to manifest in a child.

We lucked out that Taylor doesn't have it. We later learned that if both parents are carriers (as Jay and I are), the odds are 1 in 4 that a child will have SLOS. Taylor might be a carrier; she'll have to be tested when she's older.

The number of kids with SLOS is fairly low; the estimate is one in every 20,000 to 60,000 live births. But the medical community believes the numbers could be higher, because a significant number of stillborn babies might be afflicted with SLOS.

Many kids with SLOS are in wheelchairs and have experienced or will experience organ failure. They generally have facial deformities such as drooping eyelids, misshapen nostrils and lips, small jaws, and large ears. SLOS patients often suffer from vision abnormalities, seizures, heart defects, low muscle tone, bowel obstruction...the list goes on and on.

Noah doesn't have any of that. In the disability world, he's a superhero.

I truly think what made the difference is—are you ready for this—how much junk food I ate when I was pregnant with him. Remember I how much weight I said I'd gained? That was due to daily trips to McDonald's or Burger King. All that cholesterol— maybe that's what saved him from the physical conditions most kids with SLOS have.

Of course, that's not scientifically proven. But to me, it makes very good sense.

I'll tell you this: moms *know* things. We just *do*.

A MAMA'S GUT IS A BADASS GUT

CAPTAIN NOAH

When I was pregnant with Noah, I did amniocentesis, which showed that he didn't have Down Syndrome, but that was it. This is where my guilt comes in. Had they told me he had SLOS, Jay and I would have had a tough decision to make. I have no crystal ball to predict what we would have done, but I can say that if they'd told us that our child would be deformed and would likely be severely physically and mentally handicapped, we'd have given serious thought to whether or not it made sense to bring him into the world.

But again: things happen for a reason. Looking at where he is now, Noah is a miracle.

He doesn't have the physical limitations of most kids with SLOS. I asked the doctors, "Will he live a long life?"

"He should."

"Will he prosper?"

"He should."

Noah is making medical research history. The doctors have discovered he has a specific gene that other kids with SLOS don't. They think it's made him less disabled. (Although I still believe my "lots of burgers and fries during pregnancy" theory holds water, too…)

So yeah, in the genetic world, Noah is a badass.

It's only in the rest of his world that things are tough. This is because he has the mental limitations that are common for kids with SLOS. Hypersensitivity to what he sees and hears, sleep difficulties, slow mental processing. A lot of kids with SLOS have behaviors similar to what kids on the autism spectrum have, such as constant upper body movement, attachment to particular objects (that bracelet!), and hyperactivity. As it is for many autistic kids, everything is literal with my son.

Even today with Noah—he's 14 now—it's difficult to explain something simple to him, like that other people bully because they get bullied. I'll say something like, "Joey gets teased at school, so he's taking it out on you. That's why bullies bully."

And Noah will just say, "No. Joey doesn't get bullied." He's unable to understand the subtle types of bullying that some kids do.

No matter how much you try to explain something, Noah just digs in. You can't reason with him.

Noah will meet a stranger, and the first thing he'll say is, "Hey, I know all the presidents. Do you want to hear?" And he'll recite them in order. Then he'll say, "I think maybe I'm going into the Army when I'm older."

If the stranger is a kind person, they might reply, "Okay, bud."

Then Noah will ask, "Where're you from?" But before waiting for a reply, he'll say, "I might go in the Army when I'm older." It's as if he's forgotten not only that he just said that, but also that he'd asked a question and should wait for a response.

You can't really converse with him. He's not programmed for conversation.

But he just wants to fit in, and so much of what happens around him, he doesn't understand. He reminds me a bit of Forrest Gump.

Every year, Halloween is a challenge, finding someone he can trick-or-treat with. I've gone trick-or-treating with mothers I couldn't stand, but if their kids wanted to be with Noah, I happily did it.

"Who's he going to go with?" I'll ask Jay. "Who's going to be his friend?"

Speaking of Jay, he refused to help. Even once we had a diagnosis, once we had a name for Noah's condition, Jay still spent most of his time working or playing golf. I'd be there crying, and Jay showed zero empathy. Everything with Noah's care always fell to me.

But I went along with that and didn't complain, because the last thing I wanted to do was risk losing Jay again.

TO EVERYTHING, THERE'S A SEASON

In late summer 2017, when Noah got home from camp, he was grey and so skinny. It was shocking; I thought I'd have to take him to the emergency room. But that was right before we received his SLOS diagnosis, and we didn't know how much cholesterol he needed to survive. He hadn't eaten well at camp, and it showed. Once I adjusted his diet, things improved.

That fall, he started sixth grade in the special needs school, Divine Academy. He was at Divine for sixth grade and part of seventh.

He's never looked at himself as special needs. In seventh grade, he asked me, "Why am I at a special needs school?" He could clearly see the disabilities of other kids at Divine, particularly kids with physical limitations, but because he's so literal, he couldn't see his own disability.

He really wanted to go back to public school, so we decided to give it a try. And it was an unmitigated disaster. Kids would go on Instagram Live, filming him. They'd say, "Noah, cut your eyebrows!" and he would cut his eyebrows. They'd tell him to twerk, and he would twerk.

He was stealing money to give to people who bullied him into doing it. They egged him into fights with much bigger kids. They'd yell, "Fight, Noah! Fight! Fight!" And he'd fight, and get beaten to a pulp, because he's so small for his age.

We pulled him out of public school, and I home-schooled him for a few months. Then, last spring, he asked if he could go back to Divine Academy.

He's still about three years behind grade level. But at Divine, they work with him within his abilities. We're so grateful he goes to school there.

Blue Ridge Camp had always been a safe summer refuge for Noah, because it was the same camp year after year. Taylor went there, too; these days, she's a counselor at Blue Ridge, in fact. But in the summer of 2018, she couldn't go, because she had to do a summer session before she started college. We thought Noah would have a tough time at Blue Ridge without Taylor, and that a totally different camp environment might be better for him.

So we found him a new camp. It was in Pennsylvania, and was advertised as a special needs camp. Noah, Jay, and I went up there to tour the camp and meet the owner. It seemed beautiful. It seemed perfect.

Within nine days, he was home. When he made too much noise at night and disturbed other kids' sleep, they put him in a room called the time-out closet. They'd haul him out of bed in the middle of the night and put him in there.

He wrote me letters home saying things like, "Somebody here told me, 'I hope Hitler comes back to life and kills you.'" We even learned that one time, a camper used a broom to hit a counselor who was grabbing Noah, in an attempt to make the counselor let go of Noah.

It was horrible. We thought about suing the camp, but it wasn't worth going down that path. I did report it to the regional director of the American Camp Association.

The thing about special needs is, it's such a huge spectrum of things. They called this a "special needs camp" but what does that mean, specifically? We later learned the owner had never worked with special needs before. He'd bought the camp a year earlier. He didn't know what he was doing. Rule One is that you never put your hands on a camper. But they'd walk Noah, one staff member gripping each of his arms, to that time-out closet. In the middle of the night! No wonder he was terrified.

Noah spent the rest of that summer just sitting at home with me. I wasn't in a great space myself, and having him around made it tougher. I felt like I was losing my mind.

BOY IN A BUBBLE

I've had to keep Noah in a bubble. During that long summer sitting at home, I wouldn't let him go anywhere alone. But how do you keep a teenaged boy in a bubble?

One time last year, Noah told me something truly terrifying:

that he wanted to kill himself. He'd even looked up YouTube video on how to do it. He doesn't understand the ramifications of something like that. He thinks he doesn't want to be here at this particular moment, because he's sad or upset—but he doesn't understand that if he killed himself, that would truly be the end. I live in a perpetual state of fear that he'll watch something awful and then do it.

In retrospect, I wish Jay and I had more closely monitored Noah's internet and social media usage starting when he was old enough to begin spending time online. If I had any advice to give parents, especially parents of kids with special needs, it would be that. Because the more freedom you give some kids in this area, the more they're going to push back if you try to lay down restrictions. All kids need to be watched when it comes to the online world, but for kids like Noah, it's all the more important, because he has so much trouble viewing online information with a critical eye. It all just comes at him like being hit with a storm, and he takes it in without knowing how to distinguish healthy messages from unhealthy ones.

I blame myself, because I had so much going on in my own life (lots more on that in Chapter 8), and as a result I wasn't on top of Noah's social media. Noah can wear me down, and I give in. I was naïve to think Noah only played video games. If I could do it over again, I would have insisted we limit his phone to nothing but calls or texts. Could've, would've, should've. We learned the hard way.

It started out with Snapchat. Taylor told me that Noah had Snapchat and he was posting ridiculous things. We made him delete it. Then, out of left field, Noah had Instagram, and he was posting ridiculous things there.

"Just use it to look at other people's posts," we suggested to him. "Don't post anything yourself."

That sounds logical, but of course he didn't do it. He started posting live, silly videos on Instagram. We made him delete Instagram, but he later just installed it back on his phone. When I found out, I went bat-shit on Noah.

I'll be honest, I don't yet have an answer for this one. It's a minefield.

One of the things that helps me is talking to other parents who are going through the same things. There's a Facebook group for SLOS parents, and even though most of their kids have much more severe disabilities than Noah's, I still feel we can empathize with one another. Parents of autistic kids are also helpful for problem solving. And there's a moms' group at his school. They all get it, because in one form or another, they know what it's like to raise a child with special needs.

I've learned that sometimes you have to get creative to find your community. Sometimes you have to dig a little deeper to find people you really connect with.

It helps to feel like I'm not alone. To have conversations like, "Oh, my gosh. Your child does that, too? Oh, my God, are you losing your mind?" Being able to have those conversations, talk freely with someone who gets it—that's invaluable.

Noah is 14 now. We still have our struggles, but having a label helps a lot.

These days, he wants to be independent, but it's hard. For

instance, he refuses to wear a bike helmet. We've resorted to taking his bike away.

He's always had babysitters, but now that he's older, we call it Noah-sitting. We use Taylor's friends who are boys. We'll say something to Noah like, "How about if Robert hangs out with you today?"

"Cool."

These boys are older, of course. They drive, and they'll take him to the beach or the mall. But Noah thinks they're simply his friends. We've never made a big production out of paying Noah-sitters in front of Noah (though we pay them well). We used to leave money for them in the mailbox; now, we just pay them through phone apps.

One day not long ago, we had a commitment that we couldn't bring Noah to, and we couldn't find a Noah-sitter. We left him on his own, and he ventured far from home. He has an app on his phone that tracks where he is, but he found a way to disable it. I was terrified, though he made it home okay. But that's the kind of thing we have to live with daily, and it gets harder and harder as Noah gets older.

One of the things I need to do soon is research places where people with special needs can live as they transition to adulthood. I don't mean an assisted living facility, but a community where Noah could live and have someone oversee him, but still have some autonomy. I'd like him to be slightly on his own, but still protected. I want him to experience living with people besides us, if at all possible. I'd like him to experience community.

Not long ago, he said something so funny to me. He likes to wear his hair flat. To me, he looks like a combination of Jim Carrey when he was in *Dumb and Dumber* and Moe from the *Three Stooges*.

I was giving him a hard time about his hair, and he said, "Mom! This is who I am. Let me be myself!"

I had to laugh. Here I am writing a book about being true to myself—but I wasn't allowing my son to be true to *himself*.

"You're absolutely right, bud," I told him. "You be you, Noah."

What I've learned from parenting Noah is that God only gives me what I can handle. I've learned to be more patient. I've learned to accept Noah's quirkiness, to not see it as a negative.

GOD ONLY GIVES
US WHAT
WE CAN HANDLE

I've learned that trying to reason with my son depletes me, and it's not worth it. Instead, both Jay and I have learned to "speak Noah."

This is our norm. It's not normal or typical, but this has become our norm.

ASK YOURSELF...

- If you are a parent, what are your hopes and dreams for your child?
- How do you protect children from bullying? Should you step in, or let them work it out for themselves?
- What creative parenting workarounds have you come up with that make it easier to parent your kid(s)? If you do not have workarounds, can you brainstorm some with your parenting partner and/or other parents you know?

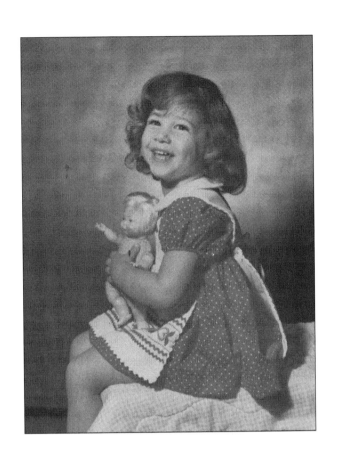

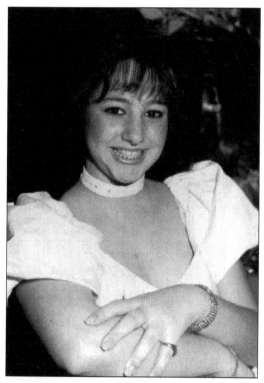

1985 and 1986 were the pictures of frizzy Marni

Lisa in the background with her jaw dropped looking at Nancy with her family thinking "That's my Nancy" and the rest is history

Dinner with Steve Wynn in 1984

TR and I were very silly and this was our lunch
break-posing

The only picture Jay and I took together before we got married is this
one, it has hidden bay hidden behind the trees.

Michaelson , Mr. Ralph Renick

My mother with Barry Gibb, New Years at Nancy's

CHAPTER 7

ALL THAT GLITTERS IS NOT GOLD

THE PULL OF ACCEPTANCE

I'm going to take a little departure here from the chronological account. I'm doing that because the issues I'll talk about in this chapter—issues around acceptance—have come up repeatedly throughout the years. It's my hope that if you, too, struggle with acceptance, what I discuss here will provide insight.

Jay said something recently that really struck me. I said to him, "I've realized I still want to prove my self-worth to Aunt Nancy. Why is it that I *still* have to prove something to her?"

And he replied, "Because they never accepted you. So many other people have embraced you, particularly lately. But to have your own family diss you like that, of course it's still hard on you."

He's right. I've been thinking a lot lately about the strong pull of acceptance. Even as a middle-aged adult, and despite how many people are supportive of me these days, I don't want my own family to see me as a failure.

It still affects me right *here*. (If you guessed that I'm pointing at my heart, you're right.)

I also think the fact that I still feel this way, all these years later, shows the depth of one human being's ability to affect another.

When it came to my family, there was a point where I had to come to terms with hope inevitably leading to disappointment. I was doing everything I could to get my family to love me, and it never, ever worked.

For example, I enjoy making gift baskets. I love to give presents. I just love it. For years, I would do that for them—put together individualized baskets for each person in the family. Or at Christmas or Hanukkah, I'd do something like take a Barbie doll and tailor it to each family member's interests, then set it in front of all their other presents.

I did those things as a creative outlet. But my efforts were unappreciated; nobody seemed to notice or care. I finally realized that not one of my family members would do something like that for me.

I had to ask myself an important question: was I doing these things only because I wanted something in return? It took much soul-searching to answer that.

There were two choices. One, I could keep giving my family thoughtful gifts, and find a way to get over my resentment when they weren't appreciated or reciprocated. Or two, I could channel that love into giving things to other people, people who would appreciate my efforts.

I chose the latter. And I've been much happier since making that choice.

"WE DON'T DO UGLY."

Nancy is 69 now, and she still works out like a maniac. She always has a perfect hairstyle and makeup. She's been that way her whole life, or at least as long as she's been with Uncle Jerry. I guess she was terrified he'd leave her if she let herself go.

Growing up, I felt so inadequate around her. No matter how hard I worked at it, I never felt I was as pretty or sexy as Nancy.

I wish the message had been, "You want to be comfortable in your own skin. At the same time, you want to have healthy habits. Not everybody's as slim as a model walking down a runway. And you don't necessarily even want to be, as long as you're focused on your health."

But there was no such message from Nancy. Instead, the only way to gain her acceptance was to look like her. And for me, that was an impossible goal.

Aunt Nancy would say, "We don't do ugly. We don't like fat."

One night when I was about 25, I was visiting her and out of the blue, she said, "I know what's bothering me."

"What?" I asked.

"Those hair extensions of yours." She made a face. "Get them out."

When I was pregnant with Noah, it was a time when I wasn't speaking with my aunt and my mother. But when I told them later how much weight I'd gained, they both said they were glad they hadn't seen me pregnant. It's like they wouldn't have been able to handle a 200-plus-pound Marni.

Nancy did all these things: surgeries, diets, tons of makeup. I look back at pictures of her and think, *this is what I wanted to emulate?*

I always struggled with food issues. When I was upset, like when Jay and I were having our affair, and he'd turn off his pager, I ate huge amounts of chips. Sometimes I couldn't eat, but more often I overate.

No one ever said: "Are you self-inflicting with food? What's your *real* pain about? What's really upsetting you?" And I wasn't self-aware enough to ask myself those questions.

If you're experiencing something like that, I'd ask you to channel it. If something is giving you anxiety—trust me, I get it. We all get anxious. We all have rough days.

But you can go for a run, or even just take a walk. If you're hungry, you can enjoy something healthy and delicious and then call it good.

We all love tasty things. Hey, I enjoy ice cream just as much as the next person. But when you're eating a treat, make sure it's simply that: a treat. Make sure you're doing it for enjoyment of the food. Don't use food as a crutch.

When I talk with girls and young women, I say to them, "Don't weigh yourself. Get off the frickin' scale. Just put on your clothes and make sure you feel great."

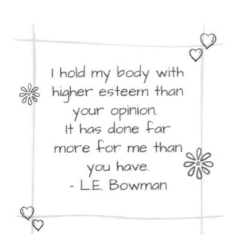

I hold my body with higher esteem than your opinion. It has done far more for me than you have.
- L.E. Bowman

I no longer go by the number on the scale, or even the size of my jeans. I just go by how I feel.

When I was young, Nancy would say, "Never go out of the house without makeup on." During the "Nancy Years," I had to be all made up, all the time. Now, I never wear makeup. I wear moisturizer, that's it. I'm usually in sneakers, with my hair in a bun.

I've learned to be me. It took a lot of years, but I'm finally happy in my own skin.

CHILDHOOD PTSD

Is there such a thing as childhood PTSD? Honestly, yes, I believe there is. I have no psychological training, but I've been through years of therapy. And I know that certain situations can trigger emotions from long ago.

Over the years, I saw this time and again in myself. If somebody told me, "I know we had plans, but I can't make it—" oh, my God, I took it so personally. But now I recognize that situations like that are simply bringing up abandonment issues from my childhood.

I did the reverse, too. If someone said to me, "Let's go for lunch," I'd think, *oh, we're best friends now!* I was so happy for any sort of positive attention—from anybody.

Sometimes I think a part of me is stuck being 17. I don't dress inappropriately, but I do like cute clothes. And when I catch a glimpse of myself in a mirror and I'm in, say, some little skort, I think, *am I still just trying to be a cheerleader?*

People tell me, "Marni, you're so fun at heart." And I think, *really? Is that it?* Or is it because I'm stuck, trauma-wise, at 17, and that's why I'm so giggly? I can do *High School Musical* with Taylor's friends and have a great time. I love it when her friends come over.

But there's this other part of me, this other internal part, that's fuming. I'll catch myself thinking, *I wish Uncle Jerry was lying in a hospital bed where he couldn't move, so I could tell him to his face how much I can't stand him.*

It's not emotionally healthy, at my age, to still think that way about someone I haven't seen in decades. It's something I'm working on. I'm learning to let go of my anger, let go of my pain.

To this day, I don't know what it's like to say "my parents." I don't have parents.

No one raised me. I just tried my damnedest to grow up.

DAGGER EYES

I used to go for the jugular, but instead of a knife, I'd use words as my weapon. And when I couldn't use words, I used my eyes.

When I was taking acting classes, we would do this exercise where one student wouldn't say a word, would just concentrate on a particular emotion, and it was supposed to come through their eyes. Everyone else would try to decipher the emotion that student wanted to get across. We were supposed to guess what they were feeling, based on what we saw in their eyes.

When I did it, they could tell right away when I was feeling anger. I could feel it, too. I know what I look like when I'm angry. I know what my eyes look like.

In my family, they used to make fun of me for having evil eyes. When I was growing up, Aunt Nancy frowned upon verbalizing upset feelings. So when I was upset (which was often), I wouldn't say anything, but it was all there, in my eyes. They'd call me Dagger Eyes.

AN UPHILL BATTLE TO PROVE MYSELF

One year when I was working at the Green Agency, we had our Christmas dinner at this restaurant called Prime 112. And that afternoon, Nancy ran into my coworker, Lisa, who mentioned our dinner that night.

Nancy said, "I'm going to Prime 112 tonight. You can't go there."

"It's our business dinner," Lisa said. She walked away, thinking that was the end of the conversation.

At the restaurant that night, my boss told Nancy, "We love your niece, Marni. We adore her." But Nancy didn't hear that. She was furious because we were at "her" restaurant.

Speaking of Lisas, there was a point when Uncle Jerry's daughter Lisa became the principal of the temple preschool that Taylor attended. I think Jerry made some huge donation, and that's how Lisa got the job. One time while she was working there, she called Nancy and told her, "Marni didn't pay her tuition."

Nancy called me. "Is there a reason you're not paying Lisa?"

This was during the years I was on my own. "Because I don't have the money," I said.

She yelled at me.

I understand people need to pay their kid's tuition, but come on. Would Nancy and Lisa have done that to any of the other preschool parents?

During that time, Lisa was dating a rabbi, so they took Jewish holidays very seriously. That year at Passover, they asked me to take Taylor, aged two, and leave the table. Nancy said, "Would you mind going upstairs? Taylor is ruining the Seder."

Taylor and I had to sit in a bedroom and miss dinner, because Taylor was talking during Lisa's boyfriend's Seder.

The following year for Passover, I made kugel and red mashed potatoes before I went to work. During the day, my mother came to my apartment, got my food, and brought it to Nancy and Jerry's. My car was in the shop, so I'd asked my cousin Ross if he could pick me up at my office and take me to the family Seder.

Unfortunately, my callback ran late. The client was Nabisco, and I couldn't just walk out. I asked Ross if he'd mind waiting for me another ten minutes.

Um…turns out he did mind. He headed to Nancy's place, and they commenced the Seder without me. They happily ate the food I'd made. Nobody would come get me.

With my family, it was just discard after discard after discard.

"YOU'RE MY DARK PLACE."

Remember how I said I lost my identity when I quit agenting to become a stay-at-home mom? As another ill effect of that, I now felt I could only prove myself to Nancy through Taylor's success. I figured I no longer had success of my own, but I *did* have Taylor. And no mother raising a daughter as wonderful as Taylor could be a screw-up, right?

Once I learned that Nancy had a phone with texting capability, I sent her tons of pictures of Taylor. Cheerleading, hip hop, all of it. Eventually, Nancy blocked her phone when I sent pictures.

When Taylor was 12, she was on Channel 6, dancing hip hop. I was beyond proud, but instead of simply enjoying the moment, I *had* to tell Nancy. I wanted Nancy to watch my daughter on TV. I wanted her to see what I'd created.

She didn't care.

Last year, I made a video about my leukemia diagnosis. (We'll be talking about that in the next chapter.) It's on YouTube, and it's had a lot of views. Taylor called Aunt Nancy to tell her about it. She thought Aunt Nancy might want to watch it. Nancy hadn't seen Taylor since she was three, so this was sort of out of the blue—but Taylor thought she was doing a good thing.

Nancy said, "Taylor, you and your mother are my dark place." She went on, "Please, with all due respect, I'm at a great place in my life, and I don't want any problems. Be well, but don't contact me again."

Nancy has had more impact on me, was more damaging to me, than my own mother was. There were a lot of years when she was the only mother figure I had. But her love was conditional: only if I looked thin, only if Lisa wasn't mad at me, only if Uncle Jerry was out of town.

Oh, I remember those days. If Uncle Jerry was away on business, Nancy would call me and say, "Marni, you're like my daughter. Come for dinner." But when Jerry was in town, the rule was, "Do not call me after 5:00. That's my husband time." You couldn't just call anytime, couldn't show up at their house out of the blue.

A few years ago, Jay and his business partner bought an old-time movie theater in Miami. The plan was that I was going to turn it into a performance venue, but retain its character. I was really excited about this project. I called Ross and said, "You gotta tell your mother about the movie theater she used to go to when she was younger. We just bought it, and I'm turning it into a beautiful performance space."

I have no idea whether or not Ross passed that message to Nancy. I never heard a word from her about it.

Thinking back, I have to ask myself why did I that. But the answer is clear: because I wanted Nancy's approval. Still.

THE GRADUATION, PROM, AND WEDDING I NEVER HAD

In 2013, I had the opportunity to participate in an incredible event. It was a fundraising gala, a charity event based on the show *Dancing with the Stars*. The judges were members of the JCC (Jewish Community Center), and three hundred people were in the audience.

My partner was a professional dancer named Shawn. His best friend, another dancer named Kathleen, was also part of the event. She was paired with another layperson (like me!). These professionals practiced with us for hours, for days on end. I learned not only from Shawn, who led me exquisitely, but also from Kathleen, who taught me the "girl stuff." I swear, Kathleen turned me into Baby from *Dirty Dancing*.

For the gala, Kathleen loaned me an outfit she'd worn on *America's Got Talent*, when she and her partner were semi-finalists. It was a hot pink dress that flared and flipped as I moved.

That outfit transformed me. Honestly, I was 43 years old, and I'd never felt as sexy in any item of clothing as I did in that dress.

When I danced at the gala, it represented my graduation, my prom, my wedding—my everything. I felt like it was *my* moment.

And yet, most people from my community were cheering for my competitor, Eric. He was a guy I'd known in school, actually, who now lived in my suburban neighborhood. It hurt that everyone was cheering for him. I took it personally.

Even so, during Shawn's and my actual performance, I felt great. When I look back now at a video of myself—wearing this little hot pink thing, dancing and flipping through the air—I can't help but smile. It was an incredible feeling.

So how did it end? Well, Shawn and I lost the competition. Some people (even some who'd cheered for Eric) said to me afterwards, "You were great. You should have won."

And I replied, "I *did* win. I went out there and danced my heart out, in front of three hundred people. To me, that's a win. I don't need a trophy."

Still, when it was over, I felt empty. Shawn went back to his life…and I had nothing. I'd wanted the feeling I had when rehearsing and dancing onstage to go on forever. I could have rehearsed every day.

In retrospect, I put a ton of expectation on this experience. I'd had the greatest time preparing for it. I love to dance. I loved the way our performance turned out. But I went too far with it, because I was expecting my community to change its thinking about me, based on the fact that I'd put myself out there this way.

And they didn't. Everyone had fun that night, but when it was over, they all forgot about it. I hadn't had a lot of friends in the neighborhood before the gala, and I didn't gain a single new one as a result of it.

It was my family all over again, except with other people this time.

Much later, I realized that while I had a great time preparing for the gala, I'd also begun to put too much expectation into it. In my mind, the hope of what might happen afterward became almost bigger than the event itself.

And then the "afterward" didn't live up to my expectations. I became disappointed, because my expectations had been too high.

What could I have done instead? I could have followed up the event by taking ballroom dance classes. Perhaps I'd have found a new community that way, a community in which I felt connection and acceptance.

Maybe I will, someday! I still have my ballroom shoes. So why not?

"True belonging doesn't require you to change who you are; it requires you to be who you are."
- Brené Brown

GREEN WITH ENVY

Remember I said I didn't have a bat mitzvah? Taylor didn't have one, either, but when she turned 13, we had a "not-mitzvah" for her. It was basically a big party to celebrate Taylor becoming a teen.

At Taylor's not-mitzvah, another mom said to me, "When I have Mathew's bar mitzvah, can you not look like that?"

Maybe she meant it tongue-in-cheek; I don't know. She was talking about the fact that I looked great in a dress that night.

But she couldn't have seen the whole picture. I'm sure the main reason I looked great was because I was so happy for Taylor. But that mom didn't know what I'd give to have a family—a mother, a father, siblings, aunts, uncles, cousins—come to my child's bar mitzvah, like the one she was planning for her son. To have family to spend holidays with, hang out with, celebrate weddings, births, and other milestones.

People you can simply depend on. People about whom you might say, "Oh, yeah, my sister's a nut, but I love her, and she loves me!"

But here's the thing about envy: it can destroy you, if you let it. I used to feel envious of so many people. I used to wish I had someone else's life.

I don't do that anymore. If I see somebody with a great ass, I don't think (or worse, say), *oh, look at Miss Thing.* Instead, I'll say to her, "Wow, you look awesome—so fit! Do you do squats?"

I'm asking you, please: never, ever bring another person down. I've been in the gutter, and it's not a pretty place. I'd never want anyone to feel the way I used to feel.

WORKING ON IT

Sometimes I'll ask myself why I care so much what other people think. I'll say to myself—*no, wait a minute. I'm investing so much in what other people think of me that I have to fight that all the time. I don't want to fight so hard about this.*

We all want people to think well of us, but you need to make sure that the people you're concerned about, the people you're concerned about whether they care about you—are they the right people? Are they people who deserve your concern?

It goes back to the ego and the soul. The fact that my family discarded me so easily, I guess it affected my ego. I was seeking approval from people who would never give me approval, and that, in turn, made me feel terrible about myself.

I'll admit it: even today, I'm not fully at peace. But I'm working at getting to a place where I feel overwhelming peace.

But it's a journey. I'd love to get to a place of peace all the time. Or at least a lot of the time. Sometimes I experience that and it's great, but I'm not there every day. Sometimes I feel it and I know I want to be there…but then I go back to a darker place. And then I'm just a broken person, a person who's working on it.

We're all working on it, right?

TIME IS YOUR ALLY

Here I am, 49 years old and still in that mindset of having to prove myself. Still hoping to be accepted by people who have been nothing but detrimental in my life. What's most impactful is that I'm still so impacted by it.

I've been trying to dig myself out of this hole for so long. I've come to realize that the longer that we try to do something like that, the harder it gets.

I share this with you in particular if you've got fewer years under your belt than I do. If you're young, you have the opportunity to recognize this stuff now. I didn't recognize it for decades, and as a result, I'm still working on it.

For you, hopefully it won't be that way. The sooner you do this emotional work, the less likely it is to scar you.

If you're a teen or young adult, and there are issues affecting you profoundly, the time to start fresh is now. I didn't do that until I was much older.

But if you're reading this now—if you're reading my words and thinking of your own situation and nodding in agreement—then now is your time. There's no better time than the present to be working on these issues.

Time, right now, is my enemy. But if you're young, it's your ally.

ASK YOURSELF...

- Are there people you're seeking approval from who might not deserve your approval?
- If you're doing things that bring you joy, who are you doing them for? Are you doing them with expectations that might not be fulfilled? If so, is there a way to do similar joyful things, but without expectation?
- If you get involved in an activity or a group, what's going to happen when it ends? How can you bring that good energy forward into something else?
- What do you *want*, as opposed to what you *need*? Remember that your ego wants, but your soul needs.

CHAPTER 8

UNZIPPING MYSELF

THE "Z GIRLS" FAMILY

I know I've mentioned a few "best times in my life" and I guess I'm lucky that I can name a few! Another one was the years when I was going regularly to a Zumba studio.

For the uninitiated, Zumba is a combination cardio-dance workout. The music is often Latin inspired, and there's a party atmosphere that's completely intentional. Other musical and dance forms are also included: jazz, African, hip-hop, and more.

I started going to a local Zumba studio, called ZFran Studio, in 2012. From the start, I was addicted. For several years, I went every morning. There was a regular crowd that was always there. "Zumba Fran" and her studio gave all of us a sense of belonging and love. We were all shapes and sizes, and the support we had for one another is something I'll cherish forever. We'd laugh and cheer each other on. We'd go out for birthday lunches. It felt like community, the type that I didn't have in my suburban neighborhood.

It felt, almost, like a family.

A woman named Lisa was part of that crowd. She called us her "Z girls"—that was the group of women who were there all the time, the people for whom Zumba was an everyday thing.

Then Lisa was diagnosed with stage four breast cancer. It happened so quickly; she was fine one day, and then—it felt like overnight—she was fighting for her life. Not long afterward, Lisa passed away.

It broke my heart. Broke all of our hearts.

We tried to keep it going, but without Lisa, the energy just dissipated. After a while, I drifted away from ZFran Studio. I tried taking Zumba classes at other places, but it wasn't the same.

What I learned from this experience is that community ebbs and flows. The Zumba family ended, and I still mourn that. But it doesn't mean I'll never again have a family of friends like they were. Something else will bring that back again. I don't know what it is yet, because my journey is still going on. But I have faith that when the time is right, it will happen.

Lisa's death was also a sobering reminder of the fragility of life. Here was a woman who was healthy, happy, and committed to fitness. And her life was cut tragically short, even though she'd been doing everything right.

If it could happen to Lisa, it could happen to anybody. Even me.

DRAMA ON THE HIGH SEAS

Not long after Lisa's passing, my family, along with another family we knew, went on a cruise. Dianne's husband, Seymour, had just died. By then, Dianne and Seymour had moved to Las Vegas, so we didn't see them much. But my own mother was very much in the picture, and she was the one who booked the cruise. She felt bad for Dianne, so she invited Dianne along.

We had three staterooms, my mother and Noah in one, Jay and

I in another, and Dianne and Taylor in the third. In retrospect, that might not have been the greatest arrangement. Dianne and Taylor didn't make the best of roomies. Dianne thought Taylor was "a mess," and she told us so, in no uncertain terms. Taylor was just acting her age, just being 16, but Dianne wasn't a fan of sharing such tight quarters with a teenage girl.

Moreover, my mother and Jay's mother didn't get along at all. They'd never much liked each other, but I think my mother figured it wouldn't be that bad, with all of us having fun on vacation. We were traveling with three other families, too, which we'd thought would ease any possible tension.

But on the last night of the cruise, it all blew up. Dianne began screaming at Taylor and throwing shoes at her.

"You motherfucking bastard baby! I hate you. That's all you are—a bastard baby. You fucking bitch. I wish you were never born. I hate you! I hate your mother!"

Taylor didn't react (I have no idea how she kept her composure) until Dianne said to her, "Your dad is poor because of you!"

That Taylor reacted to, same as most teenagers would. She called my stateroom, crying, asking if we really were poor.

"Of course not," I replied. "Don't listen to a word she says."

My mother got on the phone with Taylor and was comforting her, but we didn't know that Dianne was, at that moment, making her way across the ship. Her face beet-red, Dianne stomped into my stateroom. "I hate you! You ruined my son's marriage! I wish you'd never been born! You motherfucking piece of shit, with all your Louis Vuitton purses!"

"Oh, my God," I said to Jay. "Get her out of here."

He just stood there. Later, he told me he was in shock.

Dianne yelled, with her beet-red face, for another five minutes. That's a lot of yelling!

Then she left our stateroom, slamming the door behind her. I watched her go down the hall, away from the stateroom she was sharing with Taylor.

Noah had been invited to our friends' cabin for a sleepover that night. I knew he'd be safe with them, so I sent him over. I told him, "If you see Grandma, run the other way."

The next day felt like *Friday the 13th, Part 2*. The night had been filled with horror, and the morning was calm and serene. That was the day we docked. It was time to go home.

Jay said to Dianne, "Mom, just go to the airport. I'll send your luggage."

She got into a cab. We went with one of the other families in a van, taking us home. We were exhausted and mentally drained. Jay and I kept looking at each other, both of us thinking, *what the fuck just happened?*

At home, Noah jumped out of the van and ran inside. We dragged our tired selves and the luggage out of the van.

Noah came running out of the house. "She's here! Grandma's here!"

What the fuck? Dianne was at the top of the staircase, refusing to leave. I got in her face and yelled at her. She shoved me against the water cooler.

"We need to call the police," I told Jay. "She's crazy!"

He shook his head. "Come on, Mom," he said to her. "I'll take you to the airport."

For about a week after that, I couldn't get to sleep at night until I called her on her landline in Vegas. I know it sounds irrational, but I had to make sure she was twenty-five hundred miles away. Only then could I be assured that she wouldn't show up and murder me in my bed.

"Don't speak to her," I said to Jay. "After what she did to us—and especially after the vile way she treated Taylor—do *not* speak to that woman again."

He agreed that he wouldn't.

One Sunday afternoon the following fall, we were watching football, and Jay's phone beeped with a text message. He said to me, "Can you check that?"

It was from Dianne.

Thank you, sweetheart, for helping me win the bet on the football game. You're the best son. I love you so much.

I said to him, "Have you been talking to your mom?"

He glowered. "Fuck you! Don't look at my phone."

I was stunned. "But you just asked me to check it!"

He grabbed his phone and left the house without another word.

Oh, crap. I couldn't handle losing Jay. I called him, begging him to come home. Eventually, he did.

Abandonment, any kind of abandonment, was always a trigger for me. It didn't matter who was right and who was wrong. I just couldn't stand the idea of being discarded. So, I'd beg for forgiveness, even when I'd done nothing wrong.

SO *THAT'S* WHAT IT IS!

In December, I mentioned to Dr. Drucker, Noah's psychiatrist, that Taylor had begun to struggle. She wasn't finishing school assignments, wasn't doing chores around the house that we asked her to, would half-start projects and never finish them. Dr. Drucker recommended that I bring in Taylor for testing.

During the evaluation, Taylor was presented with a checklist.

How often do you make careless mistakes at school, work, or other activities?

How often do you have difficulty organizing tasks?

How often do you blurt out a response before a question is fully asked?

How often are you restless, as if "driven by a motor"?

The list went on and on. And as Taylor answered the questions for herself, I kept thinking about what my own answers would be.

Often. Often, often, often.

I knew Dr. Drucker worked with adults as well as children and adolescents. I asked her, "Doc, can I make an appointment for me, too?"

When my results were in, Dr. Drucker told me, "You have high-functioning ADHD."

So I went on ADHD medication. It was amazing how quickly things changed for me. I realized my house was a disaster and my husband was talking down to me. I saw how disorganized my life was, not to mention my kids' lives.

I'm not saying medication is right for everyone who has ADHD. But for me, it changed everything. I felt a clarity I'd never before experienced. When I began taking the medication, it was like I'd been in a coma and had now woken up.

I asked myself, "Why is my house so messy?" And I just spun around and cleaned it.

I became a different person. My ability to remember changed. My speech changed. I was coherent.

I was thrilled with the changes in myself. But one person who wasn't happy with my diagnosis and medication was Jay. I was seeing him clearly now, and I was speaking out, using my voice with more confidence than I ever had before.

Jay was used to me being all over the place. Not long before I was diagnosed, I needed help with my computer. I was on the phone with the Apple guy, but what he was saying made no sense to me. So I said to Jay, "I don't understand this. Will you talk to him for me?"

Jay slammed his arm on the couch, and screamed at me. "Goddamnit! Do I have to do *everything* around here?"

As with so many things, Jay figured I was just being lazy. But that wasn't it at all. I wasn't too lazy to talk to the Apple guy. I would have happily talked to him—but I couldn't follow a word he was saying.

The idea that Jay believed I was being lazy still sits with me, to this day.

Nowadays, I'm organized. I could tell you where anything in my house is. I don't know how I lived with junk drawers everywhere, with clothes in piles all over the floor.

When a difficult situation arises, I've learned to say, "I'm going to deal with it. I'm going to turn it into a positive."

Taylor went on ADHD medication, too. But when summer rolled around, she said I couldn't make her take meds at camp.

"Why wouldn't you want to?" I asked.

"Because everyone would know I'm on Adderall."

"So what?"

"Oh, my God," she said. "No."

"Is it that bad?" I asked. "The stigma?"

I guess for a teen girl, it is. At my age, it's so different. To me, it's a miracle that medication is available and has such a positive effect. If I need to be on it for the rest of my life, that's fine. I own it.

One thing that strikes me, still, is that I had no idea of the severity of my mental state until I was diagnosed and started medication.

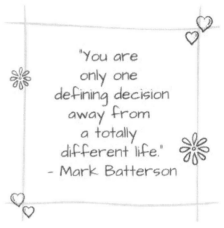

"You are only one defining decision away from a totally different life."
— Mark Batterson

I'll say this to you: *some things are not easy to see, at first glance.* But if something doesn't feel right, look into it. You never know until you explore the issue. There's so much help out there—please, if you suspect you might need help, seek it out.

It can change your life. It changed mine.

RETURN OF THE MOTHER-IN-LAW

In April, it was Jay's birthday. I never get the mail, but one day I did, and there was a birthday card from his mother. For a year, he'd been secretly talking to his mother, even though he'd promised me he wouldn't.

Not only that, but when I confronted him, he lied about it. He looked right at me and said he wasn't in touch with her, that she'd just sent him the card out of the blue, because it was his birthday.

"Don't lie to my face," I said. Then I left the room.

Look, I get it. I understand that she's still his mother. I understand why he spoke to her. But the proper way to communicate about it would have been to say to me, "I feel really bad about my mom. Can we can talk about it?"

Instead, he chose to lie. That incident began a domino effect of Jay and me pulling apart. I began to doubt everything about my marriage. It broke us; it broke a trust.

To be fair, Jay was in a truly terrible space. He had an insane mom, and he was trying to have a family and maintain a business. He was caught in a bad place.

But at the same time, he wasn't being open and honest with me. He continued to lie. The tension in our house was horrible.

I could see that things were spiraling out of control for Jay. A guy he did business with, Chris, co-owned a truck stop restaurant with another guy, and Jay started talking about buying out Chris's partner. I couldn't believe it: Jay really thought he was going to work every day at this restaurant he knew nothing about?

The truck stop thing fell through, but Jay was also working another deal with some people he knew. Some of them owned a few Dunkin' Donuts shops, and they formed a group to buy more. But then they came to Jay and said, "We want to buy you out. We don't want you to be a part of this anymore."

It was infuriating. Jay was the one who had put the group together in the first place! No one else had the connections to do that.

This was a first for Jay. Despite our personal issues, when it comes to business, Jay is top-notch. No one had ever asked him to step aside in a business deal.

I was so mad that they'd hurt my husband. I was livid about what was going on between us, but still, my heart hurt for him about the Dunkin' thing.

Later that year, Jay went to Las Vegas for a convention. At that point, things had calmed down between us, and I felt we were on a better path.

THE TRUTH IS NEVER AS PAINFUL AS DISCOVERING THE LIE.

"Are you going to see your mom when you're there?" I asked.

"I wasn't planning on it."

I was glad to hear that, but I had a gut feeling that things weren't right. I checked the phone records that night, and sure enough—there was a call to Dianne the minute his plane touched down in Vegas.

I wish he'd simply been honest with me. Instead, I had to find out by being a spy.

IN PAIN ALL OVER

One evening the next spring, when Jay came home from golfing, I said, "I don't feel good. I'm not myself."

He wasn't exactly sympathetic. He just said I should go to bed, and I'd feel better in the morning.

But by the next day, my body was in pain all over. I felt like I was giving birth.

I went to the emergency room, and they checked all the normal things. They could see the pain I was in; I thought I might die right there on the floor. They didn't see a kidney stone, but they thought it might have passed. They told me to go home and try to rest and relax. The ER doctor also recommended that I make an appointment with a hematologist.

Later that day, the ER doctor called to check on me, and he reminded me about the hematologist. I was confused about why he recommended this.

"To be quite frank," he said, "I think it might be cancer."

Stunned silence on my end.

At the hematologist's office, they ran a bunch of tests. And that afternoon, I got a call. "Mrs. Goldman, it's Dr. Martinez. I'm just calling to let you know you have chronic lymphocytic leukemia."

"What?" I didn't even know what that was.

I went to a doctor named Grossman, whom everyone said was the best in town. They did blood work again, and it was a two-week wait to find out if I was staged.

In those two weeks, I pretty much didn't get off the floor. Not because I was in physical pain—they gave me meds for that—but the emotional pain, the worry, the shock, drained me completely.

Jay and I went in to get my results.

"You're not staged. You're watch and wait," Dr. Grossman said. "You will die *with* leukemia but not *from* leukemia. So, live your life. Just be careful with sun, with your overall health. Come in every month for the next six months. Then we should be able to taper to every two months."

Dr. Grossman thinks I've had leukemia for the past eleven years. Turns out that I have three genes in an instance where most people have only two. That made me more susceptible to leukemia. But I have the "best of the leukemias," if you can call it that.

What could have given me an infection so severe it triggered the doctors to suspect leukemia? We don't know, but I think it was stress, because stress definitely affects the immune system.

VANITY TAKES A BACK SEAT

One thing Dr. Grossman insisted I do was see a dermatologist. Everything checked out, but when I asked if I could still get Botox, they told me no. "You could get an infection."

I'm not happy with wrinkles, but I've stayed away from Botox. One of the things that happens with a leukemia diagnosis is that vanity really takes a back seat. I've learned to be comfortable in my own skin, be comfortable with what I see in the mirror. I'm taking care of myself, and that's what matters most.

It's important to focus on your personal wellbeing. That includes your physical health, mental health, and spiritual health. Stress has such a domino effect. And being selfish about your own wellbeing doesn't help you or anybody else.

My leukemia diagnosis came totally out of left field. It was so random. I cried, not because I have leukemia, because it is what it is. I was mourning the loss of what I thought was a healthy body. "Wait! I'm not healthy anymore?"

It made me think about Lisa, my Zumba instructor, and how shocking it must have been for her to be diagnosed with breast cancer, when she'd thought she was perfectly healthy.

Learning I had leukemia was all the more difficult because six months earlier, we'd gotten Noah's SLOS diagnosis. I'd felt that was enough to deal with. I was stunned to find I also had health issues.

IT HURTS ON THE INSIDE, TOO

By the summer of 2018, things had gone from bad to worse with Jay. It was always lies. I guess it started with all the sneaking around during our affair. And then it was just a whole big crazy cluster of bad.

It didn't help that I got zero sympathy from him about the leukemia. It was like saying to somebody that's drowning, "It's no big deal. You're not drowning completely."

Dr. Drucker kept saying, "You need an antidepressant. It's not situational; it's an umbrella, and you fall under so many different categories."

"But I'm not depressed," I said. "I'm taking Adderall, and I have Xanax when I need it. Jay's the asshole. I'm fine."

Poor Dr. Drucker. If she could have shoved an antidepressant down my throat, I think she would have. But she couldn't force a patient to do what the patient didn't want to do.

Then Kate Spade killed herself. When it's somebody you don't know but she has a certain face in society, it's striking. I thought: *I have a daughter; Kate Spade had a daughter*.

When I thought about intentionally leaving my daughter… that thought changed everything.

I have a picture of a bunch of celebrities, with a line under it that says, "This is what depression looks like." Robin Williams, Marilyn Monroe, Kurt Cobain, and many more. People you'd never think, with their smiling faces, could be depressed.

But depression is a chemical imbalance in the brain. It can't be controlled by simply "snapping out of it."

So, I finally agreed with Dr. Drucker. And I have to say, it was the right thing to do.

It's the hardest thing in the world to admit that you have a mental health disorder. There's so much stigma around it. But denial hurts you more than it hurts anyone else.

> "There are wounds that never show on the body that are deeper and more hurtful than anything that bleeds."
> - Laurell K. Hamilton

SO LONG, HIGH SCHOOL

Taylor always said, "Ugh, it's so boring, living in the suburbs." But it was good for her. She took honors and AP classes. She was a cheerleader. She started a club called "Blessings in a Backpack," to help feed children whose only guaranteed meals are the free or reduced-price breakfast and lunch at school—which means nothing in the evenings or on the weekends, of course. Taylor graduated in May 2018 and prepared to enter her freshman year at the University of Florida.

It made me think about my own high school years. My senior year was nothing like Taylor's. I didn't go to my 30-year reunion. I didn't want to go back and talk about 1988; it was the worst year of my life.

But in some ways, I wish I had gone. Because after high school, the playing field evens out. We all put on reading glasses now. No matter if you're successful in business, or have been divorced three times, or if you had aspirations to be an astrophysicist but found you preferred teaching middle school science classes…whatever it is, the playing field is even in adulthood. Most people are mature enough to focus on the good stuff. It's not like high school, where kids look for reasons to bring each other down. High school is a tough time for a lot of people.

WHY AM I HERE?

I was happy for Taylor when she went off to college, but I missed her, too. Jay was resentful and angry about his work situation, and I was dealing with Noah. It was exhausting.

I'd say to myself: *Why am I here? Why did God put me here? I don't want to be here anymore. I'm ruining everybody's life.*

I was pity-partying. Even with the antidepressants, I continued to have suicidal thoughts. But I didn't actually want to jump out a window. When people have suicidal thoughts, most of them aren't plotting in detail how they're going to do it. Instead, it's a way of saying, *I don't want to be in this pain anymore.*

Jay and I were ignoring each other. There was no friendship, no love, no tenderness. We were both angry. I think deep down, Jay resented me for getting leukemia. As if I'd done that on purpose!

Taylor was off at college. I had leukemia. Noah had one issue after another.

I was no longer dancing in a hot pink dress. I wasn't fabulous Marni.

I was just tired.

One day I was sitting in my house alone, crying. *Why does all of this happen to me? I don't deserve this. I can't take this.*

But then I had a realization.

This is teaching me a lesson, I thought. *What is this teaching me?*

Not why is this happening to me, but what can I learn from it?

I realized that no one could fix things except me. I hadn't come this far to just come this far.

More and more, I realized that Jay had never behaved like a true partner. If somebody was rude, Jay would ask me, "What did you do?" I never felt like he was on my side.

I was shifting away from Jay. I had a great idea for a business I wanted to start. (I'll talk more about that in the next chapter.) Steven, whom I'd dated during the back-and-forth years of Jay's and my affair, had stayed in my life as a friend. Steven had marketing experience. He was helping me with branding for my business, which I called Peace, Love, Marni. He helped me design a logo and gave me advice on other specifics I needed to get the business going.

Around this time, Jay and I agreed that a trial separation was a good idea. We hadn't actually done that yet, but we were talking about it.

Nonetheless, one night Jay called Taylor at college. She later told me he was crying over the phone. He said to her, "Your mother is cheating on me."

What? Steven and I weren't seeing each other romantically—not then, anyway. It was just business. But Jay had never seen a "business Marni," so he wasn't prepared for me to become that person. Moreover, he didn't mention to Taylor that we'd been talking about a trial separation. He made it sound like I'd run off and was having a wild affair.

I admit it; I was so pissed, after that Steven and I *did* date, just a few times.

When Jay found out, he started pacing all over the room. "I'm gonna have a heart attack," he said.

"What? Why?"

"Because you're seeing someone else. You, dating another guy."

"Jesus," I said. "You weren't gonna have a heart attack all those years ago, when I was hemorrhaging and about to die on the floor. You weren't gonna have a heart attack when Noah was diagnosed with SLOS, or when I was diagnosed with leukemia. But because I'm seeing someone else, *now* you're gonna have a heart attack?"

"Yes," he said. "I can't even *think* about you with another guy."

I just rolled my eyes. Of course, Jay didn't have a heart attack. He was fine.

Anyway, with Steven it was mostly business. Once he'd helped me with the parts of my business that were his areas of expertise, we amicably went our separate ways.

CAN WE FIX THIS?

Jay and I decided that before we made the decision to formally separate, a vacation together was a good idea. Maybe it would serve as a reset, we thought. We made plans to go to San Francisco with another couple we know, Mitch and Emily.

I thought Dianne could watch Noah when we went on our trip. But Jay suggested having our handyman, Lawrence (no relation to disgusting Laurence), stay at the house instead. Jay said, "It would be much cheaper than flying my mother in, if we had Lawrence and his girlfriend stay here. Noah loves Lawrence, and he's basically self-sufficient, anyway."

The night before we left, Lawrence's girlfriend came over with him, whacked and wasted. I bitched to Jay that this yuck of a person couldn't watch Noah. He yelled at me, and I yelled back.

But it was too late to make another plan. When they arrived

the next day, the girlfriend told me, "I clean houses on the side. Can I clean your house while you're gone?"

I wasn't sure it was a good idea, but still, who can turn down the idea of coming home to a clean house? So I said okay.

Our bedroom door was shut, the way it always was when we went away.

The trip to San Francisco was great. It was the best trip I've ever gone on with Jay. We had an amazing time, and came back optimistic that things between us would improve.

When we got home, the girlfriend was in our master bathroom with the lights on and cleaning supplies on the floor. The lights were on in the guest bathroom, too, and there were some cleaning supplies in there, but by no means would I say either bathroom (or any area of our house) was clean.

I said to Jay, "What's she doing in our bedroom?"

I thought he'd agree with me that it was weird. We'd shut the door, after all. But instead, he said, "Well, you told her she could clean the house."

"But our bedroom?"

"She said, 'Can I clean the house?' And you said yes." Jay sighed. "Now you're exasperating me again. I don't have the energy to be exasperated."

But he was exasperating *me*, too! He knew she shouldn't have been in our bedroom. True, we hadn't said that specifically, but it seemed clear to me, based on the closed door.

The argument escalated from there. Jay and I sent Lawrence and his girlfriend home, and commenced yelling at each other.

I couldn't believe that little disagreement turned into something so massive. But I should have known better. A few days of vacation hadn't turned·everything around 180 degrees.

That was the last straw. I'd had it with Jay.

The next morning, I packed my bags.

ON MY OWN—AND A SURPRISE "DATING" SCENARIO

Jay seemed shocked that I was leaving—which kind of shocked me.

"Why are you acting so surprised?" I asked him. "We've been talking about this for weeks." I continued packing. "I can't take this," I went on. "No matter what, you always have to be right—and I need peace."

I got myself a little apartment about ten minutes from Cooper City. At first, Taylor didn't know I'd left. Mostly, that was because she had exams, and I didn't want her to worry. But also, I hadn't been talking to her a lot lately, because I couldn't tell her how bad things were at home. She'd worry, and she'd put it all on me, I knew…not on Jay.

I tried to do Peace, Love, Marni stuff, but I was in a place of confusion. I'd pick up Noah from school sometimes and he'd come to my apartment, but mostly he didn't want to be with me and didn't want to be at home. He spent a lot of time riding his bike around our suburban neighborhood.

Taylor finished the school year and came home, so, of course, then she learned what was going on. But she had her own priorities: seeing friends she'd been separated from during the school year, getting ready to start her camp counselor job. She was mad at me for leaving, but she was in her own world, too.

Then, without telling me, Jay went on anxiety medication and an antidepressant. I didn't learn this until later, but Jay had gone to see Dr. Drucker.

But he didn't go to get help for himself. Jay later confessed to me that he went to Dr. Drucker to ask her, "Can we get Marni off Adderall? Please, doctor, I don't think it's working."

"Why do you say that?" Dr. Drucker asked.

"Because when she's on it, I can't talk to her at all."

Hah! Of course he couldn't. That's because Adderall helps me have clarity, and that drove Jay crazy.

He said to Dr. Drucker: "I can't discuss anything with her. It makes me so damned mad at her."

"Let's talk about that," she said. "Let's discuss your anger."

By the next time I saw her, she'd started treating Jay, too (unbeknownst to me). Now that she'd heard his side, she kind of laid into me. I said to her, "Dr. Drucker, I really resent the way you're talking to me."

She replied, "I am so impressed with the way you just said that."

I've learned it's not just what you say, it's how you say it. I looked at my psychiatrist and told her, "I don't like the way you're treating me." But I said it in a gentle, nonconfrontational way, and it was very effective.

Learning to pause before I speak has brought me much peace.

I was doing okay in my own place, but I wouldn't say I was truly happy. One Friday in June, I called Jay and asked if he'd come over to help me put together a piece of furniture I'd bought. When he got there, I immediately noticed a lightheartedness about him. I was walking my dog and Jay was coming around the corner with a spring in his step.

I ran to him and hugged him.

I'd just been through a pretty traumatic experience that had nothing to do with Jay or our marriage. (Much more on that in Chapter 10.) That night, I told Jay all about it.

I was worried about how he'd take it, but to my surprise, he was supportive. He listened. He actually listened to what I said, without judgement or interruption.

It was a huge breakthrough. When I was done talking, he held me. I looked at him and said, "I love you so much. I need you on my page with me."

It was then that he told me about seeing Dr. Drucker, told me about his medications.

Later, we were going down in the elevator, and two women got on.

"Were you guys outside before?" one of them asked.

"Yeah."

She nodded. "We saw you. We were watching you hug each other, and it was the most romantic thing. We could see the love between the two of you."

Wait, what? *Romantic?* Who were these people she was talking about? It felt like a different Jay and a different Marni.

When I think back on things with Jay, one thing I realize is that we couldn't even communicate about not communicating. And actually, I think that happens in a lot of relationships—not just between spouses but also between parents and kids, business partners, whatever. You're not communicating, and also you realize you're not even communicating about not communicating.

I remember one time, several years ago, when Jay wanted to go on a trip to Europe with his friend Mitch. He said to me, "You don't mind if I go to Europe with Mitch, do you? Just a guys' trip?"

"Not at all," I replied.

Well, of course, what I really wanted to say was, *please, don't go*. But Jay just thanked me and went on his trip. And I tortured him; I called him every five minutes.

"How could you go?" I'd ask.

"You *said* I could go," he replied.

"But I didn't *mean* it!" I protested.

That's what I'm talking about. Not only weren't we communicating, we weren't even communicating about not communicating.

TRANSFORMATION

One night, not long after that Friday night when Jay came over, Taylor was visiting me in my apartment. We went for a walk, and on the way, we took each other's hands.

She said, "What will it be like, if you and Daddy get back together?"

"Well, we might not," I said.

Taylor dropped my hand.

And I said, "Hey, that's not fair. I need you to love me regardless of whether Daddy and I are married or not. I'm still your mom, and I'll always love you and be there for you. I hope you can do the same for me."

She thought about that, and then she said, "Yes. I can."

Do you remember Emily, Mitch's other half, whom we went to San Francisco with? She's had her demons, too; she was an alcoholic when our kids were in elementary school. She's in recovery now and holds her head high. We've known each other for a long time, but we weren't all that close. I never thought we had much in common. She probably didn't, either.

But after I became more vocal with my story, after I started talking publicly about my mental health challenges, Emily embraced me. And I mean that both literally and metaphorically. After I began stating publicly that I suffered from depression, anxiety, and ADHD, Emily hugged me and told me she admired me for speaking out, for helping remove the stigma.

It connected us, in a way. I might even venture to say that Emily and I are now friends.

So, here I am. Long ago, I accomplished that goal of "house in the suburbs." But now I know there's more to me than that.

I'm at a new level. This is the second part of my arc. It's the transformation of me.

You might think I want this for you—a second transformation.

I have to tell you: I don't want that.

Are you surprised? Don't be. What I really, really hope is that things open up for you the first time. I hope it doesn't take until you're almost 50 years old for you to figure out who you want to be.

This is where *I* am, but this isn't where you want to be when you're my age.

Regardless of how mental illness is labeled, the point is, if you're not feeling right, talk to somebody. If the first professional you see isn't a good fit, then find a different one. It can take time to find the right person.

Therapy can be one of the best things you do for yourself. Having somebody to talk to is priceless. But you have to take responsibility for it. And please, please, don't wait as long as I did!

If someone gives you a hard time about mental illness, remember, that's *their* problem, not yours. It's entirely possible that they wish they were in therapy themselves! Who knows?

THERE'S NO RIGHT OR WRONG WITH PEOPLE'S FEELINGS.

Listen, if somebody—whether it's my Aunt Nancy or the man in the moon—sees therapy as a stigma, that's their problem. Not mine and not yours.

Don't let what other people think prevent you from doing what's right for you.

DON'T SWEAT THE SMALL STUFF

With all that's happened in the past few years, I've learned not to sweat the small stuff. I try not to react. I try not to get angry.

Leukemia doesn't define who I am. I deal with it. I believe things happen for a reason. If I don't make a left, if I make a right instead, then I'm supposed to make the right. I believe the universe has put me exactly where I'm supposed to be at this moment. I trust the journey.

I'm not religious, but I do have a spiritual practice. I like motivational readings; they help me put things in perspective. I try to incorporate that motivation into my daily conversations. If somebody isn't in a good mood, I might tell them I hope a bad mood is the worst thing that happens for them today.

I'm much more aware now. I used to snap at people. Now, I try to think before I speak. Learning to do that has changed me.

NO ONE EVER INJURED THEIR EYES BY LOOKING ON THE BRIGHT SIDE!

These days, I'm a proponent of seeing the good in everything.

The work we do on ourselves physically, mentally, emotionally, spiritually, is a continual process. We're always growing and changing, but the work we do to become the kind of human being we want to be is a continuum.

People are who they are. I'd like to tell you that Jay is a completely different person now. I'd like to say we never argue, that we're back together and expect to be together for the rest of our lives. That would be the fairy-tale ending, right?

But life isn't a fairy tale, and the truth is, I don't know. Since that Friday night in June, Jay and I have had our ups and downs. We're living under the same roof again, but if you asked me if that means we'll be together forever, I'd say there's certainly no guarantee of that.

"No one can make you feel inferior without your consent."
- Eleanor Roosevelt

I've had to accept that Jay—like me, like everyone—is a work in progress. We're all capable of modifying our habits, but I can't make another person change.

The key is how I handle it. The key is remembering that others choose their behavior, and I choose mine.

These days, my life is more peaceful because I'm not reacting to Jay anymore. I'm no longer saying, "Jay *made* me feel this way." Whatever Jay does or doesn't do, it doesn't matter, because *I'm* responsible for my feelings.

PEACEFUL BODY, PEACEFUL MIND, PEACEFUL SPIRIT

Another thing that's happened is I now put more emphasis on physical activity. I'm back to doing Zumba. I practice yoga and I walk. These things have become important in terms of my recovery and therapy. They're also part of my mental wellbeing. Dancing, Zumba, and moving my body are direct routes to feeling good physically, but also direct routes to feeling good mentally. The more physically healthy I am, the more mentally calm I feel. And the more mentally calm I feel, the easier it is to be spiritually focused.

Creativity helps, too. I like to make vision-board collages. I take out my art supplies and spread them all over, and I can work for hours. It clears and calms my mind. I've been creating vision boards for years, but it used to be because I had too much time on my hands. Now, it's for inner peace. When I make a vision board, the cutting, the gluing, the way I put the pieces together, keeps my mind completely busy. I've found that when I have too much time to think, I obsess. And when I obsess, I'm miserable.

I've learned to fill my mind, body, and spirit with peace. If the peace gets interrupted, I pause to think about it. It used to be that if someone was rude to me, I would immediately lash out at them. But now I'll take a second to remind myself that I can't know everything going on in that person's life. There might be all kinds of reasons for their rudeness. I try to practice compassion and empathy.

Affirmations are also helpful. Whenever I run across one that resonates with me, I take a picture of it. I print them out and hang them up; I have a whole wall in my bedroom that's lined with affirmations. Many of them are in this book! Like this one:

"Every day may not be good, but there's something good in every day."
- Alice Morse Earle

Seeing something like that daily—having an actual visual on it, greeting me every morning in my bedroom—provides such a sense of peace.

Don't believe me? I suggest you try it!

All that being said, peace is something I have to work at, every single day. The journey to inner peace and spiritual health is ongoing. You have to nurture it. You can't expect it to stick around if you don't actually focus on it.

ASK YOURSELF...

- Do you adhere to the motto, "Pick your battles"? Are there situations for which you might decide to let something go, instead of getting into a fight?
- What was one good thing that happened today? Can you hold on to that good thing, and bring its good energy into tomorrow?

- In conflict, do you practice the art of "agreeing to disagree"? Instead of an impasse, can you work with the other person to answer the question, "How do we handle it?"
- If you have trouble talking to a partner, child, parent, or loved one, is it possible that you're simply unable to "communicate about communicating"? How might you improve your communication style, and how might you work with others to help them improve theirs?

CHAPTER 9

FROM SOUR LEMONS TO PERFECT LEMONADE (THE MAKING OF PEACE, LOVE, MARNI)

A PERFECT STORM

What does it take to create your own business? I can't say for everyone, but for me it was a perfect storm of:

- My newly discovered focus on mental health
- Getting involved with the National Alliance on Mental Illness (NAMI)
- Realizing the importance of community
- Speaking with teens, especially about:
  - Denial
  - Weight issues
  - Learning experiences
- Using affirmations, vision boards, and videos to share messages of healthy body, mind, and spirit

All of the above came together into Peace, Love, Marni! And how did that happen? Read on...

HIDDEN DISABILITIES

When people have physical disabilities, generally they're visible. And as a society, we tend to have sympathy for that. We see a child in a wheelchair, and our heart goes out to that child. Or we see someone overcoming a great physical challenge, and our hope soars.

But I have a hidden disability. Noah has a hidden disability.

So many people do. Millions of people suffer from mental illness. Some are being treated. Many are not. Either way, you often can't see it on the outside. Those afflicted with mental illness might appear to be completely fine. But inside, things are far from "fine."

These days, when I speak with parents, I tell them that if their kid frequently complains about stomachaches—well, think about that. Kids shouldn't get stomachaches every day. Maybe there really is something wrong with your kid's stomach, but, just as likely, your kid simply doesn't know how to express what they're feeling mentally. Maybe it's easier just to say, "Mom, my stomach hurts."

If you're a parent and your child says things like this, talk with them about it. Try to get to the heart of what's bothering them. Talk to children on their level. Be gentle and kind.

That goes for anyone, actually, not just your own kid. You know that saying, "If you see something, say something"? We associate that saying with things like suspicious behavior at the airport. But it also applies if someone you know suddenly becomes withdrawn, if you see a shift in mood. Whether it's your kid, best friend, neighbor, whoever, reach out and ask the person how they're doing.

My goal is to bring awareness to mental illness. I want people to realize that it's okay not to be okay.

When Jay and I took that trip to San Francisco, there was a woman walking down the street screaming, "Get off me! Get off me!" I started to cry.

Jay said, "I know...you want to go hug her right now, don't you?"

I nodded. "I do. I really do."

I didn't, though. And I still regret that. But this was before I'd truly begun to explore mental illness in depth.

Looking back, I wish I'd talked to that woman. Clearly, she had nobody. And I wonder what was going on. Did she have PTSD? Maybe she'd been raped. Maybe she'd faced some other trauma. She didn't need to be in jail; she needed help.

I think the same is true for most school shooters. The 2018 shooting in Parkland, Florida happened practically in my back yard. The kid who committed that horrible act didn't ask to be born that way. But he should have been in therapy. Maybe he needed to be hospitalized. He shouldn't have been in a general school population.

But what if it's *you*, not someone else, who's struggling inside?

The answer is the same: find someone to talk to. I know it can be hard, but you can't just sit there. You can't blame someone else or make excuses the way I used to. That's not action.

Action creates positive outcomes. Positive thought leads to a positive emotion. That leads to positive behavior, and from there, you get a positive result.

Unfortunately, it also works in reverse. A negative thought leads to a negative emotion, negative behavior, and a negative result.

INVOLVEMENT WITH NAMI

If I'd been told I had worth, maybe I wouldn't have felt worthless. That's why I volunteer for NAMI.

It's another one of those "meant to be" scenarios. My friend Carrie's mother had passed away, and I went to the shiva. I got to talking with Carrie's sister, Bonnie, and the subject of mental illness came up. I told her about my own journey toward mental health.

Bonnie told me she's on the board of directors for the local affiliate of National Alliance on Mental Illness. The goal of NAMI, she explained, is to raise awareness around mental illness. They provide resources, advocacy, and support for anyone struggling with mental illness.

"Would you consider doing something for NAMI?" she asked. "We have some programs I think you'd be a great fit for, 'In Our Own Voice' about people's personal stories, and 'Ending the Silence,' about reaching out to get help. People give presentations on their experiences. Some of them write blog posts for us or make videos."

"It's so weird you said that," I replied. "I just made a video about my story."

Bonnie invited me to a NAMI reception the next month. At the event, she introduced me to other board members, and I told them some of the crazy stories from my life. They said, "We love you. You'd be perfect for NAMI."

Really? I thought. *Maybe I have something here. Maybe I can help people.*

I had to become trained and certified. I did a mock presentation for my trainers, to make sure I'd be a good fit as a speaker and a presenter.

The process was educational. It caused me to go deep, to do a lot of soul-searching about my life and where my triggers come from. I realized how much I've overcome.

The fact that NAMI found me, instead of the other way around, feels amazing to me. It makes it even more of an honor.

FINDING COMMUNITY

The best community is a strong core of friends who accept each other for who they are. That small core of friends that trust you, that you trust, and who believe in one another. That's priceless. You need a place where you can completely let down, completely be yourself.

It's what we wish for ourselves; it's what we wish for our kids. I love that my daughter and her best friend have been friends since they were little kids. They're rooming together at college this year. They're like sisters.

I cherish that Taylor has this friendship. We *all* wish that for our kids. Every parent says it: "I want them to have friends. Good friends."

When I hear myself say that, I realize I'm still trying to get there myself. When I turn 50 next year, I'd love to have a few really good friends. It's a goal—I'm working on it!

The screensaver on my computer is a picture of the women from *Sex and the City*. The show's theme song is the ringtone on my phone, and my phone background is Sarah Jessica Parker wearing one of her fabulous pairs of shoes.

Sex and the City is a major obsession for me, because that show is completely about female bonding. I long for that. I guess that's why it's front-and-center on my technology, and why I still watch reruns of that show all the time.

For me, another show that's similar in this way is *Grey's Anatomy*. I don't know if you've ever watched *Grey's*, but the connection between the characters is the type we all wish for. It's like *Friends*. That's why people love *Friends*, right? We love this peek into the lives of people who are so tight with one another. Sure, it's just a made-up show, I get that, but still, I long for that.

This hits me especially when I travel alone. I'll be in a hotel room at night and I'll think, *I don't have anyone to call. Who am I gonna call and talk about my day, about what's on my mind?* I can call my husband, sure, and I do, but still, I long for a girlfriend, someone I could chat with anytime.

"Alone we can do so little, together we can do so much."
- Helen Keller

I think back to working at the Green Agency, all those years ago. The people I worked with were my best friends. I felt like a badass, being an agent. No wonder I was so happy, felt so in control—at least professionally—back in those days.

GETTING INVOLVED

One of the ways to create community is by getting involved. When I speak with college students, I talk about that. If you belong to the newspaper, or you're on the debate team, or you run cross-country, or whatever is your passion, if you integrate your-self into things you're passionate about, it creates a built-in com-munity. You'll automatically have a lot in common with others who love what you love.

Greek life is still a big deal on a lot of campuses. Before rush, when girls are all hoping to get into a particular sorority, I tell them, "If you don't get in, there's a bazillion clubs to join. You'll find your people. If you don't get into place A, there's places B, C, D, E, F, and G. You'll find your place."

The thing about Greek life is, you have to be *chosen* for it. But with so many other groups, if you love it, you just jump in and join. And they're thrilled to have you there.

When Taylor was in elementary school, she was the first girl to ever be elected school president. Based on that success, in high school she ran for president of her ninth-grade class. And she lost.

Now, Taylor wasn't used to losing. She was the type of girl who *always* won.

I said to her, "Hey, it wasn't meant to be."

Here's a proud mama moment: Taylor's response was, "You're right, it wasn't. I guess I'll join the journalism club instead."

She ended up becoming passionate about journalism. She made incredible friends. They were older, but they embraced her. She found her happy place within that group.

And guess what? Now, in college, Taylor is majoring in broad-cast journalism.

Wherever you are in your life—teen, young adult, not-so-young adult—find your people. It doesn't have anything to do with popularity. It has to do with connecting.

My daughter did her thing, and whoever gravitated toward her, great. She stayed true to herself. She developed a core group of friends, and instead of partying, she'd say, "I'd rather hang out at home with my friends."

Her best friends from home are with her at college. They'll be her friends forever.

COMPETITION? WHAT COMPETITION?

When I'm talking about Peace, Love, Marni, sometimes people ask me, "Who's your competition?"

And I tell them there's no such thing. Instead, I ask myself, *who else shares my passion? How can I support them? And how we can work together?*

It works so much better when everybody supports everybody else.

I've noticed this at large Zumba events. You have one teacher who brings this style, another teacher who brings that style. They all support each other and work in conjunction, because they share a passion for Zumba.

I've learned that if participants enjoy something, whether it's Zumba or motivational talks like I give, they want *more* of it, not less. If they get insight from a speaker who does something a bit like what I'm doing, that doesn't mean they'll ignore me. Instead, they're more likely to think, *oh, somebody else is talking about that, too. I want to learn more.*

OPPORTUNITIES...BOTH GOOD AND BAD

When Taylor left for college, I reiterated the lesson I'd instilled in her and her friends since they were in kindergarten: "Do not depend on anybody to support you. Get an education, so you can be self-sufficient. Have somebody in your life because you *want* to, not because you have to."

Taylor's opportunities are much broader than mine were at her age. And her enormous self-confidence is a complete 180 from my lack of confidence at age 19. But it's up to her to take advantage of what's available for her.

I knew she'd encounter mean girls at college. There were plenty of them in high school, too. But I've taught her that if someone is being a bully, there's a reason. Nobody simply decides out of the blue, "I'm gonna be a frickin' bitch." There's something else going on in that person's life. What's the *real* thing for that girl? Taylor may or may not be able to find out, but either way, she doesn't need to absorb that girl's meanness. No one does.

I used to know this girl—I'll call her Kate, though that wasn't her name—who had a reputation for throwing great parties. A lot of kids thought Kate was bitchy, but they wanted to go to the cool parties, so they pretended to like her.

But I happened to know another side of Kate. She once told me, "I barely know most of those people, and they know nothing about me. I don't even care about having parties. I just throw them because people expect me to."

What Kate *did* care about was that her parents struggled with enormous issues of their own, and that affected the entire family. Those were the things at the forefront of her mind, not being a popular girl who threw great parties.

When I speak to teens and young adults, I tell them, "Don't make assumptions. Understand there are reasons people are how they are. Have compassion."

Another thing I said when Taylor went to college was, "People will offer you a bunch of stuff: drugs, booze, pills. And it only takes one time trying something you shouldn't. Don't ever let me get that phone call."

You have to be true to yourself. But at the same time, you have to understand that the world is what it is. If you get in a situation where you're uncomfortable, get out. Don't question. Just walk out the door.

That goes for substances, and it goes for relationships, too. If you're going out with someone new, let your girlfriends or your mom or somebody know where you are. Make sure you have a line of communication.

You should be able to walk out the door. And you should feel safe walking out the door. But the reality is, sometimes you might *not* feel safe. If that happens, it's important that help is only a text or phone call away.

That being said, I firmly believe we need to talk with boys about this issue, too. We need to say, "It doesn't matter what a girl wears or how she acts. You still need to respect a person's boundaries."

I think a great message for boys and men is this: "Find your power in being a man who can stand up when other men do the wrong thing. Be the man who tells guys like that to quit it. Set an example—there's your power."

WANTING TO BE WANTED

I used to put so much stock in what other people thought of me, good and bad. But now, if someone is kind to me, I take it at face value. I love myself, and their kindness towards me, while appreciated, is not an assessment of my value as a person.

As a teen, I wanted love and protection…from someone, anyone. These days, I say to myself, *Marni, uh, uh. I am protecting you now.*

Look, I get how easy it is to be tempted by other people's views of us. For many girls and women, there's something intoxicating about a powerful male.

But men and boys feed off that. The captain of the football team might think, *I deserve any girl I want. We're winning football games because of me. So it doesn't matter what she wants, because I get what I want.*

He shouldn't be allowed to do that. But he'll try to, and if you're the girl his eye comes to rest on, remember this: your life is about loving yourself, not about how you come across dating the captain of the football team. Your life certainly shouldn't be about what you're willing to do in order to date the captain of the football team.

Here's the other thing about that kind of guy. When senior year is over, you're going to forget him just as fast as he's going to forget you.

Trust me—you *will*.

DENIAL

The biggest issue when I'm talking to young people is denial. They don't want to admit anything's wrong. They're afraid of failure. They're afraid of not getting that grade, not getting that job. They're putting on a façade.

I'm not depressed.

I'm not angry.

I'm not overweight. I don't have an eating issue.

I'm not underweight. I don't have an eating issue.

After I give a talk, I'm so proud of the kids who stay, who talk with me afterwards. They thank me and tell me, "I don't feel as alone anymore."

Sometimes, they send me an email after the fact: "I was too embarrassed to come up to you. I don't want people to know I have anything going on."

I write back and say, "You have as much value as everyone else who was there. What makes group A better than group B?" I also point them toward places like NAMI, where they can confidentially seek help.

Some girls don't feel worthy of boys. I tell them, "The boys need to be worthy of *you*. But you need to feel good about yourself, too."

When they're rushing for sororities, I don't want them to go in with the attitude, *God, I hope they like me.* Instead, I want them to think, *let me see if I like them.*

I tell kids who are anxious, "Just do your best and be happy. Whatever's supposed to happen will."

Taylor once told me, "My friends and I have a sisterhood. We don't care that we're called bottom tier."

"What makes someone bottom tier instead of top tier?" I asked.

She shrugged. "That's just the way it is. The top tier is popular. But they're bitchy, too."

"Well, that's dumb," I replied. "You're comparing yourselves to girls everybody thinks are bitches. But who knows? Maybe that 'bitch' just wants sisterhood, too. Maybe she doesn't care about tiers, either. Maybe she wants to be your friend, but she doesn't think you guys like her because you're calling her a bitch." I went on, "Try to get to know her. You never know."

Later, Taylor came to me and said, "You were right! I talked to this girl I'd thought was kind of mean, and it turns out she's really nice."

YOU BE YOU

Taylor has always been an old soul. I think she's so genuine.

Not long ago, there was this boy she really liked, but he didn't return her affections. Still, when he got sick, she bought him a gift basket. I was skeptical, because he clearly didn't deserve it, not from a girl to whom he wouldn't give the time of day.

But then I realized I couldn't be mad at her. She was doing the same kind of thing I've always done. She was being nice, but doing so with expectations. She expected the boy to call or say something, and of course, he didn't. And she was disappointed.

But you can't do things like that with expectations. It never works. Instead, do things that truly make you happy for no other reason than because they make you happy.

YOUR JOURNEY IS SPECIAL BECAUSE IT'S YOURS.

Here's the thing: I'm not trying to be you. I'm trying to be the best version of Marni. I won't change to fit into anybody's world, and you shouldn't, either.

What do you *really* want? What will make you comfortable and happy?

You want to be productive and creative. If that comes through pledging a sorority, great. If it comes through making gift baskets—also great.

But if you're doing it for the wrong reasons, it always backfires.

EATING DISORDERS

Interestingly, when I talk with girls and young women, I've noticed a shift. Unlike when I was a teen, few of them are tiny and skinny, worrying about their weight. Girls Taylor's age don't seem to have the food issues that girls used to have. They don't say to each other, "Let's not eat; let's go on a diet together. Let's count our calories."

I think back to when I tried to starve myself so Nancy would love me, so I'd be what Dean wanted. I don't see girls doing that as much these days, and that's a good thing. We've removed a lot of the stigma around being slightly overweight, which is great.

That being said, you don't want to go too far in the other direction. There are girls gaining weight today because they use food for comfort, to alleviate stress.

Look, I don't care if my daughter orders hot fudge sundaes, if she's happy. I just don't want her, or any girl, to eat that way because of anxiety or stress. I tell girls, "Instead of sitting home eating and Snapchatting, go walk with your friends."

Five or six years ago, when I saw myself turning into Aunt

Nancy, criticizing Taylor's weight, I nipped it in the bud. I never want her to have an eating disorder. And she doesn't. Taylor is comfortable with herself. She wears whatever she likes, whatever clothes make her feel fabulous.

That's great with me. If she's happy, then I'm happy.

LEARNING EXPERIENCES

I'm not a fan of the phrase, "This is happening to me."

Why? Because "this is happening to me" is completely out of your control. You're handing over control to somebody else, to a person who does something you don't like or to circumstances you didn't expect.

Instead, I suggest changing your mantra to, "What can I learn from this?"

When you do that, you gain some control over the situation. We can't control everything—but we can *learn* from everything.

The summer before Taylor's senior year of high school, she signed up to take an online AP government class while also being a counselor at Camp Blue Ridge. It was a lot, because she had the counselor job and she was watching out for Noah, who was at camp with her.

Early on, she could tell she was trying to do too much. But she didn't know you could drop a class like that. And she didn't want to tell me she was bombing it. She was afraid to say anything to me.

So what happened? Well, she ended up getting a D in the online class.

Later that school year, after she applied to Florida State, the admissions office called me about her application.

"What's with the D?" the woman asked. "Your daughter has straight As and Bs. Her SAT score is perfect. What happened with that class?"

I told her, and then I asked, "Does she get a grade explanation?"

"Sure." She told me what Taylor needed to do, where she could submit an explanation.

When Taylor got home, she wrote the explanation. But it was pretty simple and didn't really say what happened. I told her, "Write more. Tell them you were working a full-time job and watching your brother with special needs. Tell them you got in over your head. Tell them the truth. Be brave with the truth."

She did. She told them about her job and about Noah. She finished by saying, "Last summer, I bit off more than I could chew. I tried to do it all. But this fall, I retook the class and got an A." (Which is true.)

She *could* have gotten on the defensive. She could have said, "It was too hard. The curriculum wasn't written right. They gave me the wrong expectation and that's why I got a D."

But she didn't. She owned it.

The above story is great, but there's more to it. Taylor applied to Florida State and a few other colleges, and she was accepted at a school she was happy about, Indiana. But her "reach school" was the University of Florida in Gainesville.

She never thought she'd get in there. She got a D on a midterm in AP World History in tenth grade, and because of that, she thought her record was too flawed for UF. While Indiana is a great school, Taylor didn't want to go there nearly as much as she wanted to go to UF.

The following Friday, UF announced their class of 2022. Her

friends were over, and Taylor didn't look at her email until after they left. And then, the magic words: CONGRATULATIONS, TAYLOR! YOU ARE A GATOR!

"Mom, I got into UF!"

When she showed us the email, I think Jay fainted. Happily fainted!

And why did she get in? I'm sure there are plenty of reasons, but I think back to the grade explanation she wrote for Florida State. She had extended that explanation to become part of her essay for UF. And I'd be willing to bet that one of the reasons— one of the *big* reasons—UF accepted her was because she was truthful, honest, and authentic.

At the time, before her UF acceptance came in, I said to Taylor, "You'll be where you're supposed to be."

It's the same with rushing sororities. I tell girls, "Trust the journey. Where you're supposed to be, you'll be."

It took me so long to trust my journey. We might not know the answers, and we might not like some of the answers. But there's always, always an opportunity to learn.

I love the quote below, from the author Maya Angelou.

"When people show you who they are, believe them the first time."
- Maya Angelou

Sometimes it feels like the world is more responsive to fake people, doesn't it? But I've learned you can't force a connection. We meet the right people at the right time, under the right circumstances.

Being true to yourself, accepting of yourself, is the key.

When you put that person out in the world, that true you, the people who are attracted to that person are the people you're meant to be with.

I create my own happiness, or my own misery. It's in how I choose to handle a situation. I'd much rather choose the happy, positive side than the argumentative, defensive side.

AFFIRMATIONS, VISION BOARDS, AND VIDEOS, OH MY!

My belief in affirmations is strong. Repetitive words of positivity really click with me. When I read something that resonates with me, I'll think, yes, Marni, you can do that!

I love this one:

My journey is much more beautiful when I start at the bottom and work my way up. I've been at the bottom so many times. I just keep bouncing back up.

I'm also known for my "Marni-isms." I frequently throw them out in conver-

"It's easier to go down a hill than up it but the view is much better at the top."
- Henry Ward Beecher

sation, and also when I give motivational talks. If you hear me speak, you'll probably hear, "You've got a new story to write, and it looks nothing like your past," or "The most important decision you can make is to be in a good mood."

In my experience, negativity just kind of happens. As humans, we instinctively lean toward the negative. Positivity, on the other hand, takes practice. It requires intentionality.

It's easy to say, "Everything's wrong. Everything's going badly today." But instead, if you say, "This was meant to happen. I was supposed to…" and then fill in the blank…

How do you fill it in? Well, that depends on the situation.

A positive attitude creates a positive outcome. It takes more effort, though. It requires out-of-the-box thinking. It doesn't let you sit back and say, "Well, life sucks." Instead, you have to say, "There's a good side to this."

Then you have to find that good side, that positivity.

I'm a believer in the law of attraction. If you see it, you'll believe it. This is why I make vision boards, and why the goals I put on them come to fruition.

I made a vision board for Taylor when she was about 15. It was all about college, especially the University of Florida in Gainesville. When Taylor saw it, she said, "Stop—you just really want me to go to Gainesville."

"Well, it *is* a vision board," I said. And it came true.

When I make a vision board, I start with a poster board, then build a collage on it. I save magazines for this purpose; I cut out words and photos. Even if I don't need them right away, I save them for when they might come in handy. I've been cutting out magazine quotes and pictures for years. I have a huge bag of them. Whenever I run across a word like *heart, love, energy, spirit, live,* or *joy*, I always cut it out.

I like pictures of mountain homes, with fireplaces inside and snow falling outside. We often vacation in Vail, Colorado in the winter, and I've always thought it would be wonderful to live there. I have a vision board about that. Who knows? Maybe someday.

On your vision board, include what you love—and what you want. It's cathartic, cutting and arranging words and pictures of positivity.

A vision board is the law of attraction at work. If you see it, it will happen. If you see it, you'll believe it, and it will happen.

It works. You look at your vision board and think, *I have a goal. This will happen. I'll have that house. I'll have this business. I'll have this, one day.* The idea is that the vision board inspires you.

I believe in writing down your goals. If you have business or personal goals, put those in writing and have them in front of you every day. A vision board is like writing down your goals, but through visuals. Constructing your vision board will change your life.

I make badass vision boards. And you can, too!

I don't know what possessed me to start making videos. I felt like I had a message to share, so I just did it.

And I've continued to do it. Often, it's related to current events, especially as they involve teens and young adults. Bullying, harassment, and mental illness are big issues for me.

This book is one way to get that message out. My speaking engagements are another, and my videos are a third avenue.

As a society, we need more awareness. So many people are hurting. Whether that's due to bullying, abandonment, or other issues, I just wanted to talk about it, so I made one video. Then I made another one. And another.

When I made that first video and posted it online, it was like taking a mask off. I had no idea if anyone even saw it. But then one day at the store, I ran into an acquaintance who told me, "I loved your video."

"You watched it?" I asked.

"Oh, my God," she said. "It was amazing." She put her hand on my arm. "Your words came at just the right time for me. I don't know what I would have done if I hadn't seen your video. Thank you, Marni."

Wow. If my story inspires others, that's great. That's everything I hope for.

STARTING A BUSINESS

Have you ever seen *Real Housewives of New York City*? When I first started watching it was right around the time cast member Bethenny Frankel created her SkinnyGirl enterprise. Remembering that inspired me to go into business for myself. I find Bethenny Frankel to be a great role model, because of her business ethic and how she takes accountability. She has a realness, an authenticity, that appeals to me.

In fact, I'm so inspired by Bethenny, I recently reached out to her through a service that allows you to request a short, personalized video from a celebrity. I didn't just want that from Bethenny; I *needed* it! In my request, I told her about my business and this book, and in the video she made for me, she wished me great success with both. I'll cherish that forever.

It's that type of connection and inspiration that make something like a book or a business come together. One day last year, I was randomly scrolling through Instagram and came across a post by a woman named Angel Richardson. It said, "Do you want to become a life coach?"

Hmm, I thought. *What's a life coach?*

I took the bait and clicked through. I was impressed with the business model Richardson had set up. Not only was she coaching, she also was teaching other people how to coach. I love businesses that expand on positivity like that.

I watched Richardson's videos, then found more on the same topic by other people. But I knew I wasn't in a place mentally to do something like that. It was around the time Taylor started her first year of college. When I accompanied Taylor to college that September, Jay and I weren't speaking. I cried and Taylor drove. I was lying across the front seat of Taylor's car, crying because of an argument with Jay.

It should have been a wonderful experience, sending my baby off to college, but instead, I was miserable because of what had happened with Jay. I deprived myself of that experience.

Clearly, I was in no position to coach anyone else about their life!

2018 was such a hard year. I wanted to do life coaching, but I knew I wasn't emotionally there. I had good days and bad days. That happens to everybody (even life coaches), but I knew that my good days needed to strongly outnumber my bad days before I could consider doing something like that as a business.

But then a few months later, I remembered the woman who'd thanked me for my video, who talked about how it came along at the right time for her. And that made me wonder: *could I do something with that?*

I said to myself, "You know what? I like volunteering for NAMI, but I also want to make a living. I don't want to be beholden to my husband anymore."

I didn't even know the password for my bank account. Jay handled everything, and it was time to change that. I decided it was time to start a business of my own.

I wasn't sure exactly what my business would look like, but I had a great name for it: Peace, Love, Marni. There's a clothing company that I love called PeaceLoveWorld. I have tons of their stuff. I realized that these days, I am love, I am peace. And I wanted that to be part of my brand.

When I got in touch with Steven to help me with branding, he showed me some websites and videos of people doing motivational speaking. I thought, *I can do that, but add humor to it. Funny and spunky are my signature traits.*

For the first time since my agenting days, I thought: *I can do this.*

I told Steven, "I'm tapping into what I know. It's my world."

When I put those first few videos on Facebook, I had no expectations. I didn't expect anybody to watch. I didn't expect anyone to stop me in the grocery or email me.

But they did. I've been flooded with messages.

You're so brave.

I'm so proud of you.

Keep doing it, Marni.

You go, girl! Keep it up.

The first talk I did for college girls was at a UF sorority. It was kind of a test for me—could I do this? Could I connect with these young women?

And I did. After the talk, I realized: *I have something here.*

It's about sharing stories, about creating connection. It's a kind of therapy.

What does Peace, Love, Marni mean?

It's this: I used to walk around with the glass-half-empty, negative stuff filling my mind. I'd cry and ask myself, *why is this happening to me?* I played the victim.

But I'm not a victim. I'm human. Whatever comes my way is supposed to come my way. Learning this has brought me peace.

I am loved. I am happy. I am at peace.

So, I'm starting to get Peace, Love, Marni out there. When I thought about giveaway items that people don't throw out (or give away), one idea was umbrellas. No one throws out umbrellas, right? You never know when a sunny day might turn rainy! So I had umbrellas printed with the Peace, Love, Marni logo.

I'm working on other ideas, too. One thing that helps is that I'm not at all shy. I tell everyone about my business. I tell women, "Hey, if you have your friends over for a girls' night, have me come talk. I promise to inspire!"

Give me a stage and I go to town. I'd love to get on TV. I see myself walking across a stage, talking to people in my passionate Marni way.

I've got a vision for that—and I'm working on it!

Someone once asked me, about one of my videos, "Who wrote that for you?"

"It just comes off the top of my head," I replied. "You can't script it."

When I did a trial presentation for NAMI, I read it like a script. And it felt like a script. That worked okay for that trial presentation, but it's not really *me*.

When I was casting for a living, when I would audition

IF WHAT YOU DO DOESN'T EXIST, CREATE IT.

people for commercials, you could hear which talent had it and which didn't. When they had it, that natural ability, it seemed fluid. It didn't sound scripted.

Now I never script my talks, and I certainly never script my videos. It's much more natural that way.

FEELING BLESSED

I said to my mother the other day, "I feel so blessed."

It's amazing to me that I can say this. A year ago, I wouldn't have been able to say it.

I believe there are two key reasons for this. The first is that I've learned to pick and choose my battles. At times, you might have to choose peace over being right. You can be right or you can be happy, but sometimes, you can't be both simultaneously.

The second is remembering that whatever is supposed to happen, happens. Take a right instead of a left? Meant to happen. Miss your flight? Meant to happen. The reason might not be apparent in the moment, but it will show itself, in time.

Knowing this, living this way, means I rarely get stressed out anymore.

It's such a peaceful way to live.

ASK YOURSELF...

- What is your vision? What are your dreams? Do you have a physical representation of that: a vision board, a list of goals, a journal?
- If you're facing disappointment, what can you do to turn it around? Can you see another path forward, one that

might bring more happiness than the one you had originally hoped for?

- Who is your community? Who do you rely on? If you don't have community, what can you do to build it in your life?

CHAPTER 10

BEING UNF***WITHABLE

WE NEED TO TALK ABOUT IT

The story I tell in this chapter is difficult to put into words, but it's important. Judging by what's in the news and what I hear in my talks with girls and women, I'm far from alone in experiencing sexual harassment and abuse. I feel it's vital that we discuss it. The first step to addressing this problem is getting it out in the open.

That being said, this isn't a story about "outing" someone. Not because he doesn't deserve it, but because that isn't something I want to do at this time.

"When trauma has shaped you, try not to confuse who you had to become with who you can be."
- Dr. Thema Bryant Davis

That's not a decision I take lightly. While working on this book, I thought long and hard about it. I might, at some future time, be more revealing about the details of this story. But I'm not going to do that here.

Why? Because this book is about positivity. And there's very little positivity in this story, except for what I learned from it.

WHO IS JOHN SMITH?

Well, he could be anybody, right? That's the point. I've deliberately given him about the most common pseudonym possible.

But John Smith is not his name. If I told you his name, you'd probably know it, because he's a well-known celebrity. But in this story, let's call him John Smith.

You know what? I just had a moment! In my mind, I called him "John Smith," instead of simply "John."

Why is that important? Because using his full name, instead of just calling him "John," distances me from the feelings I had about him in the past. There was a time—and it wasn't long ago—when my mind was consumed with thoughts of "John." For me, he was extremely personal back then.

But now, he's dehumanized. He's just some guy. Just John Smith.

THE "FLIRTSHIP"

I'll spare you the details of how we met (because it's really not relevant), but suffice to say, he wasn't a boyfriend and he wasn't a friend. We had what I'd call a "flirtship." We talked, we texted, we Facetimed. That sort of thing.

This was in the spring of 2019, when I was separated from Jay. During that time, John Smith and I were texting, flirting, doing our flirtship thing. I admit it, feeling as lousy as I did about my marriage, the fact that I was, at the same time, receiving attention from a famous man helped ease the pain.

Toward the end of May, I told John Smith I had plans to be in Los Angeles. He said we should get together, so we had lunch at the Hotel Beverly Terrace.

I tell you, bragging to people back home, "I had lunch with John Smith"—it gave me a sense of being better than others. I was thinking, I'm *above you people. I'm in Beverly Hills, having lunch with someone famous, and you're sitting in the carpool pick-up lane.*

Getting attention from John Smith fueled my ego…not my soul.

Here's the catch, though: I didn't actually *like* John Smith. We had nothing in common. He's sort of funny, but not *that* funny. He's an actor, but not particularly handsome. He's nowhere near as good looking as Jay!

But it wasn't about any of that. It was about being able to tell people that I was rubbing shoulders with the rich-and-famous.

In case you haven't caught on by now, this is kind of the adult version of dating the captain of the football team, for no other reason than because he's captain of the football team.

THINGS GET UGLY

When I saw him in LA, I told John Smith, "I want to watch you film your next show." He agreed.

A week or so later, I flew to the city where he was filming. Originally, I wasn't planning to see him until the filming, the following night. But my plane was three hours delayed. We'd been texting back and forth while I waited for my flight to take off.

I got in pretty late, and I texted him when I arrived. He texted back, "Ugh, I've had the worst night with the producers. I just want you to come here." I caught a ride and arrived at his place about two in the morning.

He said, "I'm so nervous. I just want to hold you and hug you." And I fell for it.

We slept—or, at least, I tried to sleep. It was pretty weird, lying in a strange bed next to a celebrity!

I wasn't sure what he wanted, since he hadn't made a move on me the night before. But in the morning, it became completely apparent. I woke from a light sleep to the sound of John Smith grunting. He was all over me, *eating* my breasts. I am not joking; it felt like they were being devoured. There was no tenderness, no light kiss or gentle advance toward me. I'd been sleeping, and then abruptly I was being assaulted.

I pushed him off me and jumped out of bed. I grabbed my things and ran.

After I'd checked into a hotel (far from where John Smith was), I stepped into the bathroom to shower. I couldn't believe how horrific my breasts looked. They were covered in dark bruises.

I used my cellphone to take pictures. I wanted documentation of this…just in case.

HERE IS (NOT) WHERE THE STORY ENDS

That should be the end of the story, right? I should have either: 1) reported him to the police, or 2) got on the next plane back to Miami and tried to forget about it.

Guess what? I did neither of those things. Instead, I went to his filming that night.

Why did I do that? I've asked myself that a lot, ever since. All I can conclude is this: remember what I said earlier about how intoxicating powerful men can be? Despite John Smith's disgusting behavior, he was still a celebrity. I was star-struck.

Maybe, I thought, there'd been a misunderstanding. Maybe we could make amends, start over.

They were filming two shows, and I stayed for both. I hoped that afterward, John Smith and I could talk for a bit.

But after the second show, security threw me out. They said, "Mr. Smith requests that you leave."

I was furious. "Fine," I replied. "Tell him I said goodbye."

And even that wasn't the end of it. He texted me a few hours later, at 3:30 in the morning: "I told you not to come by. Please respect my boundaries."

Oh, my God. Was he serious? *I* needed to respect *his* boundaries?

I turned off my phone, gently positioned my bruised body in my hotel room bed, and cried myself to sleep.

ME TOO?

Back in Miami, I told a few friends about it. And they said, "It's assault. You can 'Me-Too' this."

I thought about doing that, but I just couldn't. I believe in good energy. I actually don't believe John Smith is an evil person. Misguided and selfish, but not inherently evil.

A few days later, I sent him a picture of what my breasts looked like. I thought he should know what he'd done.

You won't believe this—he thought I was sending him a flirty boob text.

Flirty boob text? Are you *shitting* me?

But here's the thing: I handed my life to John Smith on a silver platter. He had every scrap of power in our "relationship" (if you can call it a relationship). I had zero power, because I let myself become involved with someone who would always, no matter what, think he was better than me.

I couldn't show the pictures I'd taken the morning after the assault to Taylor; they were too awful. But I did show them to a friend of hers, someone I knew was going through a difficult time with boys.

I told her, "Don't ever put yourself in a position where this kind of thing could happen to you. If something doesn't feel right, get up and leave. I don't care who the guy is, he's not worth it."

Though she didn't see the pictures, I did show Taylor my healing breasts, a week later. She was horrified.

That same week, I happened to have an appointment with Dr. Grossman, my oncologist. They performed the standard blood tests they ran on me every time I went in. And my numbers were up. I told Dr. Grossman what had happened to me, and he said trauma can have that effect.

Of course, I also talked with my therapist, Dr. Abbey, about it. To clarify, I see Dr. Drucker for ADHD and antidepressant medications. But I also see Dr. Abbey, who doesn't prescribe medication for me. Through discussion and feedback, she helps me explore various issues I'm facing. I started seeing her years ago, when I noticed myself getting on Taylor's case about her weight, and I was worried about turning into my mother or Aunt Nancy. Dr. Abbey has been a godsend, all these years.

After the John Smith thing, Dr. Abbey and I talked about why I didn't want to report him.

"What if it had happened to Taylor?" Dr. Abbey asked.

"Oh, my God, I'd be at the police station in a heartbeat."

"Of course you would." She nodded.

(As an aside, Taylor is 19, which means that legally, she's an adult. I actually would not have been able to go to the police, if something this awful happened to her. I could advise my adult daughter, but without her consent, I could not go to the police. If I did, they'd tell me she had to report it herself. If she were a minor, I could report it, but not at her age. All we can do, as parents of young people, is maintain a foundation in our relationships with them such that if something terrible happens, they'll come to us, share with us, let us help.)

Dr. Abbey went on, "And what if it had been you—as it was—but he'd been some other guy? Some guy who wasn't famous?"

"Same thing," I said. "I'd report it in a second."

I've thought about that a lot, and I wonder if it's one of the reasons many women don't come forward right away after enduring sexual assault, especially if their assaulter is a public figure. That's what "Me Too" is about, and it's one of the reasons some people don't believe women when years pass before they tell their stories.

"Why didn't she report it when it happened?" they ask. "If she didn't report it right away, what proof is there that it ever happened at all?"

But here's the thing: there's rarely much, if any proof. It's her word against his. And he, by our society's standards, anyway, is often more powerful than she is. He has more status, more money, more privilege. She's worried (with good reason) that no one will believe her. Why should she put herself through that kind of public scrutiny?

So, she doesn't. She remains silent.

At this time, I don't want to go down the road of exposing John Smith. But, of course, there's a part of me thinking, *this guy shouldn't get away with this*. And frankly, I struggle with that. But as of this writing, I'm not making any irrevocable decisions about it.

BARING MY SOUL

One thing I *did* do was tell Jay. Remember that conversation I told you about, when Jay came over on a Friday night in June to help me assemble furniture? That was the night I confessed to him what had happened with John Smith. I told Jay the whole sordid story.

If I hadn't had that awful experience, I don't know that I would have bared my soul to Jay that night. What would I have bared my soul about? Other than John Smith, things were going okay, living on my own. I missed being with my kids, but I hadn't made any decisions at that point about my marriage.

To my surprise, Jay was wonderful about it. He held me and told me he was sorry. He was angry with John Smith, sure—what guy wouldn't be, if that happened to his wife or partner? But storming around, being irate and making stupid threats against some guy he'd probably never meet, would have been useless.

EVEN *THIS* TEACHES ME LESSONS

Another thing I've learned from all this is that I highly doubt most women and girls who experience sexual assault are hoping to get themselves some big celebrity moment. That's the assumption made by Me Too naysayers: "Oh, she just wanted her moment in the spotlight. She was holding it in until she thought she could get her fifteen minutes of fame."

But I don't believe that's true. I think one of the main reasons you don't see these stories in the news immediately after they happen is because the girls and women who suffer through them are still processing the experience. They're going through a quandary: *Okay, I know this happened. I know I've got to deal with it internally, and in my personal life. Do I really want to open a can of worms, become a public figure because of this? Do I want that to be the reason people know my name, know my face?*

I can't speak for everyone who goes through this, of course, but as for me, I'd rather be known for other things. I'd rather be known as a badass mom and a fantastic spouse, as someone who is surviving and thriving despite a leukemia diagnosis, and as a successful businesswoman and motivational speaker.

This is one of my favorite sayings:

With every action, whether it's our own or someone else's, there will be a reaction. We will react, as will other people.

We can't choose others' actions. But we can always, always choose our reaction.

UNF***WITHABLE

Pardon the language, but it sums up how I feel.

The experience with John Smith caused me to become protective of myself. When it comes to my kids, I've always been a mama bear, but through this experience I learned that the same as I'd never let anyone harm my kids, or any other kid, no one is ever gonna violate me like that again.

I hate that I had to go through what I did with John Smith in order to speak from experience about it. But honestly, the fact that I survived it has given me strength and connection I didn't have before. When it comes to sexual assault, now I can talk about it at a level beyond simply expressing sympathy for those who have experienced it. Now, I've stood in their shoes. Now, I get it.

I don't want to have that experience, but the reality is, I do, and I can make use of that. I can turn this negative experience into a positive. I can work to build awareness. I can help others, hopefully, before they get themselves in a situation like I did.

Look, I like having a pretty "shell." I enjoy being an attractive woman. But my outside has nothing to do with my inside.

The reason I got involved with John Smith is that I wasn't giving myself enough self-love or self-respect. I fooled myself into thinking there was sincerity and depth within John Smith. I did that to justify giving myself to him that easily.

I believe that if you don't have self-love and self-respect, you're more vulnerable to putting yourself in an unhealthy situation, or one that's downright dangerous, like this was.

Bottom line is this: *if something feels wrong, get out.*

You have to love yourself enough to take the actions that are right for you. No matter how great some boy or man is—and yes, some of them are great—you don't need to put him on a pedestal.

Instead, put *yourself* on that pedestal. You deserve to be up there!

I see girls looking constantly at their phone, and I know what's going on. They're waiting for a guy to text or call back. Look, I did that with John Smith. I know how it feels, when your heart is racing every time you check your phone.

Confession: when John Smith and I were having our "flirt-

ship," I thought maybe he could take this book (which was in its early planning stages then) and make it into a movie. Maybe he could take my book and make something of it.

But you know what? It wouldn't have been worth it. Not for what I went through.

Now, I've realized that if I want to do something like that, I don't need the John Smiths of the world.

I can do it myself.

ASK YOURSELF…

- What's feeding your ego? What's feeding your soul?
- If you find yourself in a position that makes you uncomfortable, what will you do? What have you done in the past when this happened, and how did you feel about it afterward?
- We all make mistakes. If you've made a mistake, what can you learn from it?

CHAPTER 11

MARNIVATIONAL MOMENTS

HOW REALLY TO DESCRIBE MARNI

Remember "161 Ways to Describe Marni M," from when I was in high school? That was a long time ago, although that painful episode still makes me sad for the girl I was. But the positive I can take from that experience is to ask: *How would I describe myself now? What* really *describes Marni M (now G)?*

I can't even put myself into words! I guess I'd say I'm a unique, fun, positive individual. At least, that's what I aspire to be.

People feed off my energy. Not long ago, I was staying in a hotel, and I ordered a room service breakfast. When the server was setting it up in my room, I said to him, "I love your mustache." He had a handlebar mustache, and I thought it looked great on him.

"Thanks," he replied. "People sometimes make fun of me for it, because it's so different."

"Well, who wants to be like everyone else?" I asked. "You stand out, and that's awesome. Be your fabulous you."

'Don't worry if people think you're crazy. You are crazy. You have that kind of intoxicating insanity that lets other people dream outside of the lines and become who they're destined to be.'
- Jennifer Elisabeth

I always look for the bright side. There's *always* a bright side.

Maybe that's what makes me what I am: sparkles, strength, and survival.

BREAKING THE CYCLE

Recently, my mother said to me, "I was a drug addict, and then I was a drug addict again. I was not recovered."

It's good that after all these years she can be honest with herself, and with me. Addiction derailed my mother for a long time. It took her many, many years to break out of that cycle. She still has good times and bad times, but overall, I think she's on the right path.

Her addiction, like that of so many substance abusers, had its roots in her incredibly low self-esteem. It's not uncommon for this to run in families. And frankly, that's scary to think about, even now, when my life is so much better than it used to be.

I'm working very hard to break that cycle, and so is Taylor. The fact that Taylor witnessed me breaking the cycle while she was growing up will, I believe, help her become a healthy adult. It will help Taylor become a confident, supportive mother herself someday—if she chooses to have a family, of course.

"You can't go back and change the beginning, but you can start where you are and change the ending."
- C.S. Lewis

I hope that if Taylor has a daughter, she'll take the best of her own upbringing and make it even better. Maybe sometime in the far future, Taylor's own daughter will do the same with *her* daughter.

And things will just keep getting better and better.

These days, I'm very comfortable in my own skin. But it's a long process. Little by little throughout the years, I've been chipping away at this.

I used to have such a venomous mouth when I was angry. The things I'd say… I can't believe it, looking back.

I'd even put terrible things in writing: "I hate you, I hate you, I fucking…" I look at that now and think, why would I put that in writing? Everyone gets upset sometimes, but what's the upside to preserving that, hanging on to it? Nothing. It's like giving someone poison, but you're the one getting sick. You may think that you're hurting somebody else or pissing them off, but really, all you're doing is hurting yourself.

I've learned to keep my mouth shut, unless there's an upside to what I have to say.

I come from dysfunction, but I know I was put on this planet for a reason. And I believe part of the reason I'm here is to speak aloud about what I went through, and how I got through it.

When I talk about Nancy, sometimes I still get upset inside. But I'm working really hard on that one. I'm learning how to let it go.

Recently, I was talking with my mother, and she was all worked up about the Nancy thing. I said, "Calm down. It doesn't matter what Nancy did. Today is the here and the now. I don't care about what she did to me. I feel sorry for her, actually."

"New beginnings are often disguised as painful endings."
- Lao Tzu

I went on, "I'm not here to dwell on what happened with Nancy. I know you're upset for what I went through. But I don't care. That happened. It's done. I need to focus on what I'm doing today, and so do you."

FINDING PEACE

Some things still make me really sad. For instance, Jay and Ashley never reconciled. He tries; he still texts her weekly. But she never responds.

Over the years, he did everything he could to reach out to her. But having a mother who was a divorce attorney and a father who'd left her for another woman—I guess I can see why, with that type of influence, Ashley wasn't interested in having a relationship with Jay. It would have been great if Ellen, seeing firsthand in her professional life how other people's children cope with these tough situations, might have thought it in Ashley's best interest to maintain a relationship with her father. But I get why it would be hard, when it's your own kid.

Jay could have gone to court, but early on in their breakup, Ellen had all the resources. He knew he'd just be throwing money down the drain. Eventually, Ashley was old enough to make her own decisions. She even changed her last name to Ellen's last name.

I can't remedy the situation, but I never forget the fact that in choosing to be with me, Jay gained the family we've created together...but he lost a daughter.

I feel bad about that, with all my heart.

Just before we separated last spring, I said to Jay, "I could never write a book about our life, because I'd have to lie about our affair. I'd never want you to look bad."

But when I really thought about it, when I started planning this book, I realized that while I didn't want to make Jay look bad, I could hardly leave our affair or anything else that's happened between us entirely out. My relationship with Jay is part of my story of survival.

Last June, when I said as much to Jay, he replied, "You know what? I own it. It's part of your story."

It's the same with Taylor. When I told her about my ideas for this book, she said, "Tell it all. That's your history, and mine. It's where I'm from." She went on, "I'm not embarrassed. As long as it's the truth, say whatever you want to say."

DON'T EVER DO ANYTHING BECAUSE YOU FEEL YOU HAVE TO. DO THINGS BECAUSE YOU WANT TO.

My nineteen-year-old has more wisdom and confidence than a lot of people decades older than her. Talk about a proud mama moment!

A WORK IN PROGRESS

I've never met another Noah. If you'd told me a few months ago that my son would try vaping, I'd never have believed you. Getting in a fist fight? My precious little Noah? It's mind blowing.

But the reality is, Noah is growing up. He's 14. He has a disability, but that doesn't stop his body from growing. And his mind, in its own Noah way, is growing every day, too.

He just wants to be a typical teenager. It's impossible to prevent him from associating with typically developing teens. Some of those kids might be starting to understand cause and effect, might understand the consequences of their actions. But those ideas are difficult for Noah to wrap his head around. Unless we keep him prisoner in our house, there will always be a risk that he'll get in over his head sometimes.

What Jay and I *can* do, however, is try to stay on the same page when it comes to Noah. Regardless of what happens in Jay's and my relationship, we're both Noah's parents. And we both acknowledge that we have work to do, as far as raising Noah is concerned.

We've both learned to "speak Noah." That means we use extreme clarity.

For instance, my mother recently took Noah to Target, and they were buying a shirt for him. He wanted to get the small.

"But you need a medium," my mother told him.

He was relentless, adamantly insisting on the small. Finally, my mother called me. I heard the exasperation in her voice as she described the situation.

"Put him on," I said.

I explained to Noah that Nanny wanted to get him the medium because he was going to camp, where he would grow, and the small shirt would not fit for the entire summer. He understood my explanation, and agreed to getting the medium. Once he processed it, with clarity, it was all good.

Details comfort him, so we try to provide as many as possible. When we fly, Noah wants to know which airline, which row we're sitting in, what type of plane, in which lounge we'll wait for our flight…and on and on. He'll track the flight the entire time.

You can't say to Noah, "Don't worry about it." There's no such thing as, "It doesn't matter." Everything matters to him.

Noah doesn't understand the phrase "over there." I can't say, "The TV remote is over there. Will you bring it to me in the kitchen?" I have to be more specific: "Behind the TV is the remote control. Please bring it to me in the kitchen." If there are more than two steps involved, he won't (or can't) do it.

One time, I mentioned the song, "Don't Rain on My Parade." Noah wanted to know what that meant. Rain? Parade? What are they talking about?

It's funny, but at the same time, it's relentless and exhausting. Noah is a work in progress, every day.

But you know what? In my own way, so am I. So is everyone.

TRUE TO MYSELF

Despite all the personal growth I've experienced, I still don't have a core best friend. I have a million acquaintances and some people I'd call friends, but I'm not super close with anyone outside my family. But I love having people in my life.

The fancy-schmancy stuff is unimportant. At 49 years old, I don't have the energy for that. I see pictures on Facebook from the dancing charity event six years ago, and at this point, I can just think, *wow, that's a great picture.* I no longer feel regretful about it, like I'm missing out on something. I know I can't pose my legs that way anymore, and I sure don't have the hair extensions I had back then!

But it's all good. I love the me I am today.

I hope that by discussing it, by giving motivational talks, I can save some of the people I talk to the agony of what I went through. The agony of feeling like other people are better than you.

It's funny, I look at the kids I've known since Taylor was in kindergarten, these kids who have grown up together. When I saw them at Taylor's high school graduation, it occurred to me that many of them had the same personalities at eighteen that they'd had at five. A lot of them, it seemed to me, still had the same insecurities they'd had on that first day of kindergarten, saying goodbye to their parents at the classroom door.

If you sometimes feel you're not "good enough," I urge you to ask yourself why. Why would you think someone else is better than you? Because she seems to have more friends? But maybe you're a person who's not into having a big social life. If so, that's totally fine. It doesn't make her "better"—it just makes you unique.

It goes back to what we talked about earlier: *you be you.*

I used to change myself to accommodate every person I met, situation I encountered, or place I had to be. I changed who I was until I realized I'm most comfortable wearing sweatpants, with my hair in a bun. That's me.

You might love to dress up in fancy clothes and heels, with lots of makeup. That's totally fine, too, as long as you're doing it for yourself. Not for someone else.

If you do something for the wrong reasons, it will backfire. Years ago, I didn't know I was conforming myself to others' ideas of who I should be. I was knocking myself out doing things for people who didn't appreciate my efforts at all. I *thought* I was doing it to be creative and kind. But I was fooling myself. Looking back, I see I was doing it for acceptance.

You don't owe people. You don't owe anyone an explanation. You don't want to be rude, but there's not a thing wrong with saying, "I'm sorry, I'm not able to make it. Something came up; can we reschedule?"

It may be a bit daunting, thinking about doing that. You worry you'll lose a friend. But you have to have enough confidence in yourself not to worry about whether anyone is mad at you. As long as you're kind, any reasonable person will understand. And if they're being unreasonable, you might want to question whether you want them in your life in the first place!

Do things because you want to, not because you think you need to. That's the very definition of being true to yourself.

These days, I practice a lot of self-care. I do that to protect myself. I know that sometimes I'll still get hurt, but thinking positive thoughts, reading affirmations, taking care of my body—all of these things help keep me from getting hurt on a deep emotional level.

Look, I still mess up sometimes. Everyone does. I'm going to mess up, and that's okay. If I learn from it, it's not a mistake, it's a lesson.

Someone might say to me, "You had an affair."

Yeah. I know.

"You have a lot to deal with, having a kid with a genetic disorder."

Yeah. Tell me about it.

"You used to seem so angry and miserable all the time."

Yeah. I know I did.

"One time, I overheard you yelling at someone. The language you used—wow!"

Hah, I'm sure you got an earful! But I'm in a much better space now, thanks.

I've had my not-so-great moments. But I've learned from them. And I've moved on.

Just this past year, I asked my first Zumba teacher, Fran, if she'd teach a Zumba class at a fundraising event I was helping organize. "You don't need to do anything except teach the class," I said. "I'll take care of the promo and everything else. It will be great exposure for your classes. It's on Sunday, the ninth."

'To be happy you have to make peace with your past, love the present, and feel so excited about the future." - Marisa Peer

"Well, that's my birthday," she replied. "But I've been thinking about a Zumba birthday anyway."

"Great!" I said. "It would be fabulous if you'd do it."

She agreed, but then she got upset because another Zumba instructor was also on the flyer. The other instructor was upset, too. They were each upset they weren't the headliner.

I emailed Fran. "I'm sorry about the mix-up on the flyer. We have to redo it anyway, because we have to change the event date. I've learned that I have to take Noah to camp on the ninth. Can we switch the event to the thirtieth?"

She wrote back. "What about my birthday? I accommodated my plans for your event."

The old Marni would have written back something sharp. I

would have been resentful, and maybe blocked her. But instead, I said, "I'm so sorry this affected your day. That wasn't my intention. Noah's been getting caught up in a lot of bad things around here, and the only place to keep him safe is camp. I love you, I miss you. Much love, Marni."

I've learned how to handle that kind of stuff without getting upset. It's a wonderful space to be in!

BEING MARNIVATIONAL

If a woman my age, a mom or whoever, is looking in the mirror and it seems like she doesn't like what she sees, I tell her, "You're gorgeous. Put on something you love. Look how beautiful you are."

What could possibly have made her think she wasn't? Probably the fact that someone told her that. Someone told her she wasn't pretty enough. Wasn't good enough.

Listen: toxic is toxic, whether it's a sibling, parent, friend, spouse, or whoever. If a relationship is bringing you misery and jeopardizing your health, if it compromises your peace, then it's too expensive. It's not worth it.

Remember that when you walk away from someone or when someone walks away from you—it's not the end of your story. It's the end of their character's role in your story.

Being yourself is the best impression that you can make.

"The secret, dear Alice, is to surround yourself with people who make your heart smile. It's then, and only then, that you will find Wonderland."
- The Mad Hatter

I happen to have a high energy level, but that's me. If you happen to be somebody who's quiet and shy, you want people in your life who embrace that.

You don't have to put on a face to meet the face. You don't have to be something that you're not. The people you love and who love you will accept you the way you are.

FULL CIRCLE

You might not believe this, but Jay and I recently sold our house in the suburbs and moved back to Aventura. We're in a gorgeous high-rise building, and I couldn't be happier.

Not long ago, I stepped out onto the balcony of our new place, with my phone in my hand, and began recording a video. Slowly, I panned all around Aventura Circle.

I could see so many of these places I've lived. My life was laid out for me, right here for the viewing from my own balcony.

Far off to the right, I could see Treasure House, where my mother, Andy, and I lived with Stanley Michaelson during the happiest years of my childhood. The apartment complexes where my family lived when I was small, where my mother, Andy, and I lived for a while, and where I lived with my grandfather when I was 17, were not visible—but I knew where they were. I could see The Hamptons, where Mafia Milton had set up my mom. I saw the building where I'd lived with Dean when we were married. The Bay Club, where I lived alone with Taylor after I left Dean, was visible. Far to the north was Hollywood Beach, the site of the small apartment where Jay set me up after my eviction from the Bay Club, where I lived when he married me for three months, then divorced me but continued seeing Taylor and me on the sly. (Yikes, remember him rollerblading over?) Much closer to where I stood on my balcony, I could see the building where I'd lived briefly with Jason, before I realized the extent of his abusive issues.

And right in front of me was Aventura Circle, the same Circle I'd been walking on the night Jay told me he couldn't re-marry me and buy the house in Cooper City with me. The same Circle I stormed home from, called a friend for support, and then called Jay back and laid down the law—which got my family into that house in the suburbs, all those years ago.

What a ride I've had! It's incredible to think about it, and to see the physical evidence of it right in front of me, a panoramic view of my life story, from my own balcony.

But you know what? As incredible as my story is, it's still history. I can't change any of it. All I can do is learn from it.

And I can live in the moment. In fact, it's safe to say that learning to live in the moment has been my salvation.

Who knows what's to come? All I know is, I'm in a great space—mentally, spiritually, and physically—to deal with whatever life hands me next.

MY COLORFUL STORY—AND YOURS!

Sometimes I just stop and think, *damn, I've been through a lot. I'm pretty badass.*

Despite the rough times in my life, I feel so blessed. Not that everything is perfect, but I'm at peace.

I don't feel sorry for myself. I don't feel an ounce of sadness.

I feel actually quite fabulous. The bad times got me where I am now. How lucky I am, to have such a colorful story!

What about you? What's your story? And are you ready to begin a fresh new chapter of it?

I hope so. I wish you peace and love on your journey!

ASK YOURSELF...

- What things have you had to "let go"? Are you at peace about that letting go? If not, what can you do to get there?
- How can you support the people around you? If you do so without expectation, how will that enhance your own life?
- What would your life look like if you were "true to yourself"? How would it differ from the life you have today?

APPENDIX: RESOURCES

Below are some resources I hope you find helpful.

Peace and love,
Marni

- **Peace, Love, Marni**. I'm here for you, anytime.
  - https://www.peacelovemarni.com/
  - Email: marni@peacelovemarni.com
  - Facebook: https://www.facebook.com/MarniG
  - Instagram: peacelovemarni
  - YouTube: PeaceLoveMarni Marnivations

- **Crisis Text Line**. Free, 24/7 support for those in crisis.
  - https://www.crisistextline.org/
  - Text 741741 from anywhere in the U.S. to text with a trained Crisis Counselor

- National Suicide Prevention Lifeline. A national network of local crisis centers that provides free and confidential emotional support to people in suicidal crisis or emotional distress 24 hours a day, 7 days a week.
  - https://suicidepreventionlifeline.org/
  - 1-800-273-TALK (1-800-273-8255)

- **National Alliance on Mental Illness (NAMI) Helpline.**
  A free, nationwide peer-support service providing information, resource referrals and support to people living
  with a mental health condition, their family members and
  caregivers, mental health providers and the public.
  - https://www.nami.org/find-support/nami-helpline
  - 1-800-950-NAMI (1-800-950-6264)

- **Childhelp National Child Abuse Hotline.** Dedicated
  to the prevention of child abuse. Offers crisis interven-
  tion, information, and referrals to thousands of emergency, social service, and support resources. All calls are
  confidential.
  - https://www.childhelp.org/
  - 1-800-4-A-CHILD (1-800-422-4453)

- **National Domestic Violence Hotline.** Reach advocates
  24/7/365 to get the support you deserve. No names, no
  fees, no judgment, just help.
  - https://www.thehotline.org/
  - 1-800-799-SAFE (1-800-799-7233)
  - Chat online at http://www.thehotline.org

- **Schizophrenia and Related Disorders Alliance of
  America.** Promotes hope and recovery through support
  programs, education, collaboration, and advocacy.
  - https://sardaa.org/

- **Substance Abuse and Mental Health Services Administration (SAMHSA).** Agency within the U.S. Department of Health and Human Services that leads public health efforts to advance the behavioral health of the nation. SAMHSA's National Helpline is a free, confidential, 24/7, 365-day-a-year treatment referral and information service for individuals and families facing mental and/or substance use disorders.
  - https://www.samhsa.gov/find-help/national-helpline
  - 1-800-662-HELP (1-800-662-4357)

ACKNOWLEDGMENTS

Dear Oprah,

I am so humbled to have this glorious opportunity to let you know deep from the bottom of my heart and soul what you have meant to me. I remember the exact moment in 1987 when I first saw your presence. You captivated me in such a way, I felt the love and compassion. You were this angel that was placed in front of me that day. I love you for everything you represent!! You have taught me to embrace my uniqueness, and writing this book, I was able to turn my words into wisdom. Thank you for being my Queen.

Darren Star, I don't even know how to thank someone who created the most iconic character(s) and a TV show that changed my life. Sex and The City, and creating Carrie Bradshaw around Sarah Jessica Parker, who I adore with all my heart, is beyond fabulous. The darkest times of my life suddenly became much brighter when I was able to watch my friends, Carrie, Charlotte, Miranda, and Samantha. The relationship the women shared, gave me something to live vicariously through. There is piece of us of me in all four of these magical women.

Michael Patrick King, I have watched the commentaries so many times, I am in awe of your brilliant creative mind. Someone recently asked me if I was really this obsessed with Sex and The City, and naturally I answered, Absofuckinglutly!

To every character that has been on Greys Anatomy. I Love You All! You were my world when I didn't let anyone else in. I was able to escape my own pain, which became month after month after month. It was my escape and happy place. Krista Vernoff, present day, thank you for bringing awareness to Mental Health in the shows storyline this season. Millions watch (obsess) and I'm sure you will be saving many. Thank you!

Hoda Kotb! I love you so much! You smile every morning is pure sunshine! Your quotes on Instagram start my morning every day! There needs to be more Hoda's in the world! Your realness shines through! Your sweetness is infectious. It makes everyone's heart smile watching you and Joel with Haley Joy, and Hope Catherine. Absolutely beautiful.

Bravo and all my Housewives! I love you ladies! Watching your lives from day one, it turned me into a bravoholic! I have learned what it means to Own it, take accountability, how to hustle, and what a step and repeat is. I have cried with you, laughed with you, waited hours in line to catch a glimpse of anyone. I own it, I'm obsessed!
Bethenny, the minute I saw you, I became a forever fan. Our backgrounds and beliefs are so similar, I related to you on a completely different level. Watching you start with $8000 in the bank

and building an empire is astounding. My daughter was 8 when the show started, and she was able to see what a hard-working independent woman you are, which has inspired us more than you know. Thank you for all that you do. #bstrong

RENT and WICKED! Two shows that changed my life! I've lost count how many times I have seen each one. When the cast of RENT sang Seasons Of Love to Bryant Gumble on The Today Show, my jaw dropped, and I was hooked. No Day But Today! Thank you Jonathan Larson.
The character of Elphaba in Wicked got to my core. I never been so deeply connected the way Elphaba has resonated with me. Idina Menzel and Kristen Chenoweth, there aren't enough words. Breathtaking and spell bounding seems like an understatement. Stephen Schwartz, your music changed me. Thank you.

Allison Janney and Anna Faris. I don't think I would be able to write this book with peace and love in my heart if it wasn't for watching the two of you. The show Mom, for the first time in my life, showed me about love and acceptance, and I was able to laugh and finally accept my own mom. The entire cast is so hilarious, and brilliantly portrays the way subjects that used to be taboo, can now be comical. Thank you, hours and hours of laughter.

Mark, Cynthia and Colin. What an amazing journey this book has been. You brought my dream to reality, and helped my vision come to life. From the very first phone call, Mark you have been so kind, sweet and supportive. This book takes my breath away. I am so honored to have Graham Publishing as part of my book and journey. Putting this book together has been such a beautiful healing cathartic process. I have loved every second of this part of the journey. Colin, you have been amazing! Thank you all from the bottom of my heart. Its everything I wanted and more.

To my Taylor Reece, My Boo Boo, My perfect Angel, My mini me. January 3, 2000 was the most amazing day of my life. I became a mommy. I am so grateful God chose me to be your mom and best friend. I know at times I was sunshine mixed with hurricane. Being able to stand here, holding my baby girl, showing you everything we overcame is truly extraordinary. Always have a person to dance it out with. Continue to sparkle and shine! Remember, you get it from your mama! "Adabacooa coo coo"

My precious Noah Aiden, My miracle, My Rockstar! Sometimes superheroes come disguised as little children. You are definitely my hero. You beat the odds! Every day I become more and more proud of the young man you have become. You taught me about staying true to myself, and I love how you remind me of that every day! The Titanic, George O'Malley and Politics. I love you more than all the sand on the beach, and all the stars in the sky.

To my beautiful mother, what a fabulous story you gave me! You are a warrior! I don't know what I would have done raising Taylor and Noah without you. I love your thinking, I was the surrogate, and these children are yours and your world. They worship their Nanny. The best thing about writing this book, was the compassion, love and understanding I came to know and love even more about you. As an adult, we are the best of friends. I wouldn't trade one second of the past, it brought us to where we are now.

Jay, I love you so much for allowing me to expose our true, raw, unconventional story. It has been a rollercoaster. Sometimes we wish we didn't meet the height requirements to get on, but boy has it been worth it. Enough to write an outstanding book about it. What we share, what we created is so rare and unique. Day by day, moment by moment. Almost 21 years. Insane! Sitting in the wrong parking lot for a half hour, major hint! 242424

All the worlds indeed a stage, and we are merely players. I love you!

.

Made in the USA
Lexington, KY
24 November 2019